The Many Faces of Special Education

Their Unique Talents in Working with Students with Special Needs and in Life

Beverley H. Johns, Mary Z. McGrath, and Sarup R. Mathur

Mary Z. McGrath

ROWMAN & LITTLEFIELD EDUCATION
A division of
ROWMAN & LITTLEFIELD PUBLISHERS, INC.
Lanham • New York • Toronto • Plymouth, UK

Published by Rowman & Littlefield Education
A division of Rowman & Littlefield Publishers, Inc.
A wholly owned subsidiary of The Rowman & Littlefield Publishing Group, Inc.
4501 Forbes Boulevard, Suite 200, Lanham, Maryland 20706
http://www.rowmaneducation.com

Estover Road, Plymouth PL6 7PY, United Kingdom

British Library Cataloguing in Publication Information Available

Library of Congress Cataloging-in-Publication Data

Johns, Beverley H. (Beverley Holden)
  The many faces of special educators : their unique talents in working with students with
special needs and in life / Beverley H. Johns, Mary Z. McGrath, and Sarup R. Mathur.
      p. cm.
  Includes bibliographical references.
  ISBN 978-1-60709-100-4 (cloth : alk. paper) — ISBN 978-1-60709-101-1 (pbk. : alk. paper)
— ISBN 978-1-60709-102-8 (electronic)
  1. Inclusive education—United States. 2. Special education—United States. 3.
Mainstreaming in education—United States. I. McGrath, Mary Z., 1947- II. Mathur, Sarup R.
III. Title.
  LC1201.J64 2010
  371.9—dc22   2009030715

♾ ™ The paper used in this publication meets the minimum requirements of American
National Standard for Information Sciences—Permanence of Paper for Printed Library
Materials, ANSI/NISO Z39.48-1992.

Printed in the United States of America

To special educators who use their talents both at school and in their personal lives and continue to enrich their schools, families, and communities with their unique gifts.

Contents

Foreword   vii

Introduction   1

1   Myths about Special Educators   5

2   Tolerance   15

3   Empathy and Active Listening   25

4   The Ability to Build Relationships with Students   37

5   Recognition of Positive Actions   47

6   Addressing Discipline Challenges   59

7   The Ability to Create Individualized Educational Plans for Students   71

8   The Ability to See Progress in Small Steps   79

9   The Ability to Adapt   91

10   The Ability to Focus on the Individual Needs of Others through Ongoing Assessment   103

11   Problem Solving   113

12   Collaboration   121

13   Advocacy and Empowerment   131

Contents

14 Family Support 143

Conclusion 153

About the Authors 161

Foreword

During the 1930's and 1940's, the psychologists and educators at the University of Minnesota developed many different scales for measuring personality, aptitudes, and attitudes. Undergraduates routinely completed these scales along with other course requirements. This was, of course, in the days before "informed consent." In 1953, as part of my introductory educational psychology course, I completed the Minnesota Teacher Attitude Inventory. I and my fellow students responded to statements like "Well-prepared lesson plans motivate student efforts to achieve" by marking a five-point scale ranging from "completely agree (5)" to "completely disagree (1)." I was pleased that my overall score indicated a positive attitude toward my chosen profession and prospective students.

In the late 1950's, I took the MTAI again as part of the requirements for my master's degree. I took it again in the early 1960's as I worked part-time on my doctoral degree while teaching emotionally and behaviorally disordered students in the Minneapolis public schools. Each time my score was lower! None of my professors said anything to me about my apparently increasingly pessimistic view of my ability to educate students, but I felt embarrassed about this worsening attitude toward the work I felt I was carrying on with success and satisfaction. I brought my concern to my adviser, Dr. Bruce Balow. Bruce was a wise and kind man who became a lifelong friend. He pointed out that when I took the attitude inventory as a relatively inexperienced teacher in training, I probably marked items like "Well-prepared lesson plans motivate student efforts to achieve" as "completely agree." After ten years in the classroom, I might have marked similar statements "agree" or "cannot decide." He explained that this was not uncommon. "I guess," he said, "like many other teachers, your real-world experience has tempered that initial optimism. Don't worry about it until you begin to mark every positive statement 'completely disagree.' If that happens, you may want to rethink your long-range career plans."

I have maintained what I believe is an emotionally healthy attitude of tempered optimism throughout my years of teaching children and adults. I continue to be amazed at the potential for learning of students in the face of exceptional challenges. Much of the public criticism of our schools reflects a failure to understand the realities of classrooms where even well-prepared lesson plans do not motivate Bob or Sue this particular morning and a failure to appreciate the tempered optimism with which Bob and Sue's teacher skillfully adapts her or his lesson plan to meet them where they are today.

I respect and admire teachers who bring "well-prepared lesson plans" to their classrooms every day and skillfully adapt them, or even abandon them, so as to meet the learning needs of their real-life students on that particular day.

The authors of this book have pooled their rich experiences to advise teachers how to maintain their mental and emotional balance while daily practicing a demanding profession. Classroom reality is not sugarcoated in this book. The attitudes and techniques suggested are those that successful teachers have used throughout their careers to avoid "burnout" on the one hand (self-blame for failures to meet expectations) or abandonment of effort on the other (blaming students for failures to meet expectations). Some of their suggestions help teachers cope with difficult situations. Many enable teachers to forestall such situations. Together, their suggestions will help classroom teachers continue to "completely agree," or on especially difficult days at least "agree," that teaching with all its challenges is an always interesting and deeply satisfying career choice.

Frank Wood
retired from the University of Minnesota as Professor Emeritus

Introduction

Those who enter the field of special education are a unique group of individuals who come to the profession to help and support those with special needs. We believe that these educators are a talented group of individuals with many strengths. We believe that these individuals should be highly valued in today's society not only for their talents in working with children with disabilities but also for the talents they bring to the world around them. Those talents serve them well in their everyday life.

This book is for special educators to assist them in realizing their many talents. It can also be used in preservice and in-service to review and discuss the characteristics of successful special educators. The role of the special educator has been identified as a complex one and is an issue that must be addressed (Wasburn-Moses, 2009). This book focuses on the skills that special educators exhibit that result in their ability to rise to the challenge of this complex role.

With the passage of the American Recovery and Reinvestment Act (ARRA) in 2009, significant additional dollars have been earmarked for the Individuals with Disabilities Education Act. These dollars must be obligated by school districts by September 30, 2011. There are specific stipulations about the conditions under which these dollars can be spent, and school officials must proceed cautiously in their spending efforts. The IDEA dollars are to be used to build services for students with disabilities within the framework of the current law.

With these additional funds comes renewed attention to the important role of special education and the hope that some of these dollars will be used for professional development for those individuals who are working with students with special needs.

School districts should use this opportunity to nourish the growth and success of their special educators and to provide positive support to these critical individuals. School district administrators should spend their time in positive efforts to utilize the money for special education. They should avoid falling into the trap of attempting to manipulate these dollars for other purposes; there has been the promise that close monitoring will occur on this money to assure that it is used for the specific purposes for which it was designed. It will be up to special educators to work with their school districts to monitor whether or not the dollars are being utilized to improve programs and services for students with special needs.

Officials at the state level should see these dollars as an investment in the future of our schools and follow the specific requirements that are part of the stimulus package. If dollars are not used for the purposes for which they were provided, chances of future increases in funding will be compromised.

One of the recommended uses of the dollars is focused professional development. Special educators should work to participate in the planning of this professional development, and school district personnel should assure that it is meaningful and relevant to those who work with students with special needs.

These funds should be considered an investment in the quality delivery of services for students with special needs. These funds should be an investment in special education teachers, giving them the tools they need to exhibit the dispositions outlined in this book.

Each chapter in this book discusses a specific disposition that is seen in the successful special educator, how that disposition is important in working with students with special needs, and how that disposition is an asset in the everyday life of the special educator.

This book focuses on the strengths seen in successful special educators and how those strengths contribute to their success in working with individuals with disabilities and also in their daily contacts.

Unfortunately we hear negative statements made about special educators—"oh, they can't teach children who work at grade level," "they only work with a few children," "their job is really easy." This book dispels those myths and celebrates their talents.

The inclusion movement has added ambiguity about the professional role that a special educator has in a school community and has had a somewhat negative impact on the views that are held about special educators. Often people are so focused on the importance of the child being included in the general education classroom, they don't value the specialized, intense instruction that the special educator provides. They don't recognize the importance of increased individualized attention provided by a nurturing individual. They don't recognize the critical dispositions that make the special educator an integral part in the school community and the importance of their work with children with special needs.

Those who enter the special education profession should be recognized as unique and necessary contributors to each child, to the school community, and to the broader community.

This book is both motivational and reflective for special educators—hopefully resulting in the reader's recognition of his/her many strengths and talents.

REFERENCE

Wasburn-Moses, L. (2009). An exploration of pre-service teachers' expectations for their future roles. *Teacher Education and Special Education, 32(1)*, 5–16.

Chapter One

Myths about Special Educators

Suzanne has taught special education students with significant developmental disabilities at the intermediate level for twenty years. She has weathered many attitudinal storms in her school district. Some teachers have commented that her job is so easy because her students can't do a lot of high-level academic tasks. Others have said that she must have a lot of patience to teach and reteach. One year she had four students, but she had no assistance. A number of the other teachers in the building would comment about what an easy job she had that year. Of course, none of her four students could be left without supervision, so during that year she had no break, no lunch, and had to develop very strong kidneys. Another year she had four of ten students who were not toilet trained.

Some of the teachers in her building commented that Suzanne was just a glorified teacher's aide—after all, teachers shouldn't be spending their time with toilet training.

Some teachers actually questioned why she wanted to work with students with such low skills—after all, should these children even be allowed to go to school?

Yes, she had heard it all, and she had spent a great deal of time working with her colleagues to provide them with a better understanding of the needs of her students. In order to integrate her students into general education classes, she worked hard to assist the general education teachers with their students. She learned the importance of working together with the teachers in her building and has been successful in changing their attitudes over the years.

Her colleague, Maria, works in the same building as Suzanne. They have developed a strong professional relationship. Maria's position in special education is considerably different. She is a resource teacher for students with learning disabilities—she provides specialized instruction to students when she takes them from the general education classroom—and at least two periods of her day she co-teaches in general education classes. Maria has also faced many challenges. Throughout the years, new teachers have come in the building and thought they could just send their students to her for tutoring. Other teachers commented that she was just enabling her students because there was nothing wrong with them—they just were not trying hard enough and were lazy. The first year she co-taught with the fifth grade teacher, the teacher was excited to have her as an aide in her classroom. Like Suzanne, she has worked to dispel the myths associated with her position over the years.

Suzanne and Maria are facing their biggest challenge this year. A new principal has been assigned to their building. The new principal, Mr. Barnett, has very little knowledge about special education and is uncomfortable having Suzanne's class in his building. He tries to get her class moved but to no avail. He does move her room as far away from his office as possible and further away from the restrooms. When Suzanne tries to explain that her class needs to be close to the restroom, Mr. Barnett isn't interested. He tells her the job she has is easy enough, and he is concerned that his other classes be close to the restroom. He tells her that since she only has five students this year, he is reassigning her aide to a general education class, since that class has twenty-five students.

Mr. Barnett doesn't seem to have an understanding of students with learning disabilities and thinks that Maria's caseload of eighteen students is way too low, and he believes she must have too much free time and assigns her to supervise two study periods with the general education classes. She explains that her students' IEPs must be followed, and she cannot allot time for two study periods. He is not happy with her and decides that she should reschedule all the IEPs—after all, those students look normal and there really is nothing wrong with them.

Suzanne and Maria worked to educate Mr. Barnett about the different needs of their students. Mr. Barnett agrees not to change Maria's schedule until the new IEPs are convened. During the fourth week of school, Maria's IEPS are scheduled, and Mr. Barnett sits in on some of them. He learns a great deal about the multiple needs of Maria's students through the reports from the parents, Maria, and the general education teachers who really depend on Maria to work with the students. He begins to understand why Maria needs to see her students the amount of time that she does.

During the fifth week of school, Suzanne is very ill one day and needs to go home around 9:30 that morning. Mr. Barnett is unable to get a substitute and can't find anyone in the building to cover Suzanne's class. He therefore has to take over the class—he doesn't worry because he doesn't think they can do much anyway. Suzanne reviews her schedule with Mr. Barnett so he knows what he should do. Within the first hour he learns that one of her students has individualized math instruction to prepare him to go into the general education classroom the second part of the hour. In the meantime, one of the students needs to use the restroom. Mr. Barnett explains that it isn't time to go to the bathroom—the student has an accident in his clothes. Another student is very upset about the change in routine and has a seizure. The whole day is a juggling event for Mr. Barnett, and by the end of the day, he is exhausted.

When Suzanne returns the next day, he explains that he will be asking for an aide for her classroom.

Throughout the years, Suzanne and Maria spent a lot of time working with their colleagues and the public to overcome the attitudinal barriers that still exist in the field of special education and that they witness frequently in the schools. At times, they felt devalued by colleagues or misunderstood by their principal, but they educated others on the importance of their position and were and continue to be proud to be special educators. They believe in what they are doing, so it is easy for them to dispel the myths that they have encountered through the years.

Special educators throughout the country face some of the issues that Suzanne and Maria face. When they hear or experience these attitudinal barriers, they have two choices. They can either begin to devalue their own profession and allow others to destroy their image, or they can choose to be proactive and educate others about the critical role that they play in today's schools. They can question what they are doing, or they can stand up for the special education profession. They can question whether they should have chosen to be general education teachers or be proud that they chose to work with students with disabilities and to provide the specialized instruction their students need.

Those within the field of special education should stand up and be proud of what they do. They must continually work to dispel the myths that they encounter by educating those individuals who make such statements or who show by their actions that they really don't understand the valuable position that special educators play. If the members of our profession don't stand up for their career, who will?

Overcoming these attitudinal barriers can be very difficult because in the real world of the schools or in the real world of teachers' organizations, special education teachers are in the minority—they are clearly outnumbered by the general education teachers. Because they are in the minority, it is sometimes difficult for them to stand up for their profession.

One of the real problems that special educators face on a daily basis is the feeling that they are all alone and others don't understand their role. Suzanne

and Maria were lucky to have each other to discuss issues related to the special education profession. They sought each other out and shared concerns and engaged in problem solving. There are instances where the special education teacher is the only individual who is working with students with disabilities in his or her building. As a result, that special educator will need to seek out other special educators within the district or special educators who come to their school building some of the time—the speech/language therapist may visit the building two days a week or there may be other special educators in a different building within the district. The special educator will want to network with other special educators through mailing list servers or through professional organizations.

In order to dispel the myths about special educators, the individuals working to dispel those myths must feel confident in their role so that they can educate others. They must feel pride in being special educators so that they stand strong for their role. The special educator cannot allow himself to be demoralized or put down by other people. Special educators must stand proud of what they do.

In the remainder of this chapter, the various common myths that exist will be listed and information about how to dispel such statements will be discussed.

MYTH: YOU MUST HAVE A LOT OF PATIENCE TO BE IN SPECIAL EDUCATION

This is actually a nice myth about special educators. When individuals make this comment to special educators, they are meaning it as a compliment to the individual. This author was always flattered when she heard this but didn't really believe that she did have a lot of patience. There were certainly many areas in her life where she did not exhibit patience.

Perhaps that perception of patience is exhibited by special educators as an understanding of the strengths and weaknesses of children with special needs. That ability to recognize and understand those strengths and weaknesses allows special educators to build on each individual child's strengths and work with the child where he or she is and build on his or her skills.

That perception may be as a result of the special educator's respect for the individual needs of each child. That perception may also be the result of the special educator's recognition of the dignity of each individual regardless of the significance of his or her disability.

Good special educators recognize the individual beauty of each student and know the importance of treating each student with special needs with respect and dignity. If these are indications of patience, the special educator does indeed possess these qualities.

At the same time, there are many areas where a special educator is not and should not be patient. When individuals violate the rights of their students with disabilities, special educators are not patient. They stand up for the rights of their children—they don't want to see the children for whom they deeply care mistreated or taken advantage of in their schools.

They lose patience when other teachers don't want to work with their children—they believe that their students have a right to be included in general education classes to the maximum extent appropriate. They lose patience when others talk about their students as if the students are not present. They lose patience when discrimination occurs against their students. They lose patience when others don't believe that their children deserve access to and progress in the general curriculum or don't deserve access to extracurricular activities.

Patience does not mean that you can be "run over" or taken advantage of—good special educators stand up for what they are doing and don't allow colleagues or others to ignore them or to devalue their profession. They must continually educate individuals about the importance of their work and the worth of the individuals for whom they provide a free, appropriate public education.

MYTH: YOU HAVE SUCH AN EASY JOB

Because the special educator's caseload of students is often lower than the caseload of the general educator, the position is often seen as an easier one. Effective special educators know how to juggle the teaching of multiple subjects, they know how to provide structure and routine, they know how to get the job done without all of the necessary tools that they should have. Therefore, they actually make the job look easy when indeed it is not at all. One of the authors ran a school for students with significant behavioral disorders, and people often commented that she made the position look easy. However, when she left, two people had to be employed to replace her and both of those individuals left the district because they said the job was too difficult.

There is also a misperception that because students in special education may have difficulties learning or might not be able to learn as quickly as the general education students, that the special educator does not have the academic preparation to complete that the general education teacher has to do. Some individuals perceive that the special educator doesn't do much work with the students. They believe that the special educator has a lot of free time during the day and doesn't have enough work to do.

In fact, the special educator is very busy working directly to meet the specialized needs of the students within his/her classroom, he or she is working cooperatively with families, working to adapt the general education instruction, and is doing all of the paperwork that is required of special educators.

MYTH: YOU ARE JUST A TUTOR FOR STUDENTS

The general education teacher often sees the special educator as a tutor in the areas that the general educator wants the student to be tutored. The student may have difficulty with science or social studies in the classroom and can't get the work done in the general education classroom where the student is integrated. The student may not have gotten his homework done. The general education teacher then sends the unfinished work to the special education teacher to finish. The general education teacher might also expect the special education teacher to provide follow-up to the instruction the teacher has provided.

While certainly the special education teacher can and should incorporate the general education curriculum, they should be providing specialized instruction to meet the needs of the student. They may be teaching the student appropriate note-taking strategies for the social studies class or may be teaching mnemonics to a student to help him/her remember key science information. However, that is beyond being a tutor. It is being a specialist who assesses the needs of the student, determines what specialized instruction is needed, and delivers that specialized instruction, preparing the student for access and progress in the general curriculum. This is a much more complex role than that of a tutor in a specific subject area.

With the response to intervention movement, the special education teacher's role in some districts is changing and the special educators are expected to work with students without disabilities, tutoring those students in their areas of difficulties. While it may be appropriate for the special educator to provide assistance to the general education teacher in data collection and in consulting about scientifically based interventions, it is not appropriate for the special educator to reduce services for students with disabilities on their caseload in order to provide tutorial services for students who have not been identified as needing special education services. In fact, it raises questions when special education teachers pull struggling general education students into groups of special education students because it suggests that these students are receiving special education services without having been identified as a special education student.

Special educators must be very cautious that they are not sacrificing the education of the special education students that they are supposed to be serving and that they are not giving special education services to students not identified as having disabilities.

MYTH: YOU ARE JUST A GLORIFIED AIDE

The author can remember when a superintendent contacted her and said that one of his general education classes was too large and he wanted to put the special education teacher in the class to be her aide and call it "co-teaching." The author took the time to explain the skills and the role of the special education teacher. She also took the time to provide an explanation of the appropriate use of "co-teaching."

Unfortunately, such instances still occur today and some special educators allow themselves to be aides while saying that they are co-teaching. A great deal of work has been done about the appropriate use of co-teachers, and careful planning must be conducted for it to be successful. However, it is not appropriate for the special educator to be an aide in a classroom. The special education teacher is a credentialed teacher with specific expertise in specialized instruction for students with disabilities.

MYTH: YOU DON'T NEED TO KNOW MUCH ABOUT ACADEMICS—AFTER ALL, YOUR STUDENTS CAN'T LEARN MUCH

When school personnel have curriculum review committees, they may often exclude special educators because they figure that the special education teacher really doesn't do too much academic work with his or her students. This is a fallacy because special educators work hard to teach their students appropriate academic skills at their level—some of their students may not achieve at grade level but still are to be exposed to academic work. Special education teachers teach math, reading, writing, science, and social studies to their students.

Students with disabilities can learn. They may need different specialized instructional techniques to learn how to do math and reading and other academic tasks. Some may have difficulty processing information delivered. Some may learn at a slower rate and need a different pace of instruction. Some may need more repetition.

Good special educators believe that they must assess the way the student with special needs learns and their specific academic levels. They then plan instruction that is appropriate to the individual needs of the student and instruction delivered in the way that the student learns best. They recognize that their students have the right to be included into general education classes to the maximum extent appropriate. They work hard to include their students into the general curriculum as much as possible.

Many students with disabilities can do academic work at or above grade level. Some students may have disabilities that impact reading, but they are well above level in math or science or social studies.

Special educators establish high expectations for their students and work with their students to meet those expectations.

MYTH: YOU DON'T NEED TO BE INVOLVED IN THE SCHOOL'S MEETINGS FOR SCHOOL IMPROVEMENT

As a result of No Child Left Behind and the reauthorization of the Individuals with Disabilities Education Act, more students than ever before are included in state assessment. Only 1 percent of the students with the most significant cognitive disabilities can be excluded from the state assessment, and they are still required to participate in an alternate assessment. In some states, another 2 percent may participate in alternate assessment based on modified academic achievement standards. Other students with disabilities are included in statewide assessment with accommodations or without accommodations. This has caused school district personnel to realize that special educators who are delivering academic instruction to students must be included in school improvement plans.

Special educators bring a wealth of knowledge to the school improvement table. They are skilled in individualized assessment and are also skilled in the delivery of specialized instruction. They are problem solvers. They also know how to adapt instruction and can be an invaluable resource in any discussions about how to improve curriculum and instruction. Students with disabilities are to be provided access to and progress in the general curriculum.

The IEP team determines the extent of that involvement in the general curriculum. The special educator can then assist school improvement teams in reviewing the general education curriculum and instruction and is a valuable resource in ways to present that curriculum to students with disabilities so that the students can gain meaningful benefit. Their wealth of knowledge also benefits those students without disabilities who may be struggling within the classroom.

MYTH:
YOU ARE JUST ENABLING STUDENTS WHO ARE LAZY

Unfortunately, students who have "invisible" disabilities such as learning disabilities or emotional/behavioral disorders are often accused of being lazy.

A common complaint is that the student with a learning disability is just not trying hard enough—if he would work at it a little more, he could do it.

There are still many people who do not understand the serious nature of a learning disability or an emotional disturbance. After all, the children look normal, so why should they be struggling with learning? Some of the students with learning disabilities look exhausted while they are at school because it takes so much of their energy to work on academic tasks that are difficult. We all know how tired we are after we have done something that was difficult for us—we aren't lazy, it is just that difficult tasks take their toll on us.

A student may have depression. Because of that depression, the student wants to escape and sleep in class or the student does not respond. Some individuals accuse that student of just not trying and engaging in sleeping to get out of the work he or she is expected to do. The student may genuinely want to participate in the classroom activities, but the significant nature of the depression may prevent the student from doing so.

MYTH: THERE IS NO DIFFERENCE BETWEEN WHAT SPECIAL EDUCATION TEACHERS AND GENERAL EDUCATORS DO— GOOD TEACHING IS JUST GOOD TEACHING

Unfortunately there are many misconceptions about the differences in the roles of the special education teacher vs. the general education teacher. The general education teacher is concerned about providing curriculum and instruction to a large group of students. Because of the diverse group of students in today's classrooms, teachers must deliver differentiated instruction to meet the needs of the group. They must also provide accommodations to those students with disabilities.

The special education teacher delivers the specialized instruction that the individual child needs. He or she plans an individualized program that is based on the specific goals of each student.

As an example, Amanda is a student who is in fifth grade and is only reading at the second-grade level. The special education teacher plans and delivers specialized instruction in reading. She has learned through assessment that the student requires a systematic, multisensory approach to learn to read. The special education teacher works with Amanda two periods per day on that systematic approach—one of those periods is one-on-one instruction. The remainder of the day Amanda spends in the general education classroom. The general education teacher works to differentiate instruction—she has other students within her class who are struggling with reading. When she delivers a social studies lecture, the general education teacher uses many visuals and always reads the visuals to the students. When she provides math instruction that involves word problems, she pairs a good reader with a struggling reader. She also provides specific accommodations for Amanda—on Amanda's IEP it has been recommended that Amanda have tests read to her.

Instruction for a student in special education must involve specialized instruction and accommodations. In today's society, some educators have lost this concept. They are busy accommodating students and have forgotten that the student in special education requires specialized instruction. If a student like Amanda can't read and we only provide accommodations for her and don't also teach her to read in the specialized way that she will learn to read, we have done a major disservice to Amanda—we have failed to educate her.

The general education teacher is unable to deliver specialized instruction because he or she does not have the time or training to provide specialized instruction to the student who needs special education. The special educator can work with students individually or in small groups, can thoroughly assess, and can plan and deliver the specialized instructional techniques that the student needs.

SUMMARY

Special educators must continue to dispel the myths that surround the profession. They must continually educate those around them about what they actually do and the many skills and talents that are required of them. They must also dispel the myths about the needs of their students. They must continually advocate for the individual needs of their students and educate individuals about the nature of the specific disabilities their students have. They must stand proud of their profession and their many contributions in education.

Chapter Two

Tolerance

Susan is a principal of an inner-city urban school. She has 700 students in her elementary school, most of who come from families of diverse cultural, ethnic, and socioeconomic backgrounds. She really believes that every child has a right to the best possible academic instruction. As an instructional leader, she keeps academic excellence as a priority in her school. She ensures each student in general education as well as in special education receives the best educational experience. She puts an extra effort into hiring wonderful teachers and paraprofessional and support staff, and she encourages all of them to attend professional development workshops.

Parents in general are supportive of her leadership and agree with her views. For example, some parents consider academics as an essential means for future success. For others, however, it means that their children are able to receive the appropriate individualized instruction they need. They want to make sure that their children are receiving an education from a qualified and knowledgable teacher who is sensitive to their needs. Susan works very hard to ensure that all children receive the appropriate education they deserve.

Mary is a coordinator for the special education services in this school. She is responsible for providing mentorship to the special education teachers in the district. Beth is a special educator, and she runs a multiage resource classroom. They both appreciate Susan's leadership and find her to be supportive of special education. Recently, the district decided in favor of inclusive practices for students with all mild to moderate disabilities. As a result, students with significant learning and behavioral challenges will have to move to another school in the next academic year. Mary and Beth are currently serving children with autism, mild to moderate cognitive disabilities, and other behavioral challenges, and all their students will be moving to Benz Elementary School in the fall.

To be prepared, Mary has started going to Benz Elementary School where she will be working with two teachers to help them in establishing classrooms for children with special needs. The principal of that school is Stephanie. Biased against special education, she thinks that children with disabilities only need care and not teaching.

Mary has a tough time asking for resources and convincing Stephanie that these children need effective instruction. However, academic instruction is becoming a dividing point between Mary and the principal of Benz. Parents want their kids to have access to the best possible education because they were used to having it in the previous school. For Stephanie, however, it is not a high priority. Should Mary tolerate this type of thinking of her principal? What does she need to do?

DEFINITION OF TOLERANCE

Tolerance is defined as "an ability to recognize and respect diverse practices or beliefs" *(American Heritage Dictionary*, 2000); in other words, it is freedom from insularity or prejudice. However, it does not mean letting leadership ignore relevant and meaningful goals for individuals and schools. The above example of Mary indicates that she may have to educate her new principal, Stephanie, and assist her in getting rid of some of her prejudices against special education.

Knowledge comes from what we have been taught or have experienced. Prejudices and biases are also part of our knowledge. Indirectly or directly, we often learn to be biased or prejudiced. Without a sound understanding of individual differences, of various cultures and beliefs, and of the importance of individual rights for freedom, we educators fail to model tolerance in our own actions. We become narrow-minded. Stephanie is one example of that.

In addition to lack of knowledge, another factor that interferes with tolerance is a push for standardized procedures and outcomes. Although one of the purposes of standardization is to bring uniformity and consistency in outcomes for all, it generally creates inequities that result from widening a gap between what is expected of the student in a specific context and how the student learns in this context. As a result, standardization creates a barrier for both the general education and special education systems to effectively accommodate the needs of learners. Schools that fail to recognize the need for differentiated instruction for students with special needs and push for certain approaches to teaching take away flexibility, an essential ingredient of differentiated instruction.

Schools need to create a context of professional learning, where leadership personnel, general educators, and special educators come together to learn about children with special needs and their individual differences and unique qualities.

Some other factors that contribute to the bias against special education are political agendas, nature of funding, inadequate administrative support, and lack of professionalism. Another problem is that instead of viewing special education as a fully developed discipline, many people view it as a glorified child care system. Special educators are often told that meeting the needs of one child with disabilities means denying the needs of ten other children, and it creates an ethical dilemma in a political environment, where the special educator has to change his or her role from being an educator to a politician. Schools expect more and more from special education teachers without investing much in them and their children.

So the special education teachers not only need to advocate for children with special needs but also they need to constantly educate professionals around them and make sure they are not viewed as too reticent, as not taking sufficient initiative, as inadequately creative in teaching children with disabilities. It's tough to tolerate some of these apprehensions while at the same time to be understood well by others.

Tolerance Is Strength, Not a Weakness

Tolerance reflects flexibility and open-mindedness. Educators must display tolerance and respect for students from various backgrounds and be a model for others on how to be unbiased; they must show the moral and intellectual courage to accept the rights of others to have different values, traditions, and lifestyles.

Tolerance goes beyond commitment to human rights or respect for rights of others; it includes teaching toward social justice and equity.

In the learning environment, without mistakes and errors, there is little augmentation of ideas and minimal innovation and originality. Flexible teachers are approachable and put forth the extra effort to help their students learn. In order to make sure that no child is left behind, special education teachers are on the lookout for new, alternative, unconventional ways to teach students math, reading, writing, science, and social studies. They show flexibility by providing individualized attention in a classroom full of children and know how to create opportunities to teach in various ways for the diverse learners they encounter. Without this flexibility, a quality education is no longer an achievable goal for many students in special education.

NEGATIVE EFFECTS OF INTOLERANCE

One should know what happens in learning communities and schools when intolerance takes over. Uncomplimentary language that devalues, demeans, and depreciates certain groups, cultures, or sexual orientations emerges.

Stereotyping begins, and groups of people are described negatively. People begin to attend to specific human behaviors, attributes, characteristics, and attires so as to ridicule or insult; and people are viewed on the basis of stereotypes rather than on the actual facts or specific behaviors. As a result, certain groups of people are excluded from social benefits and opportunities.

Special education has gone through a similar cycle of intolerance starting from denial, neglect, and exclusion of students with disabilities from educational environments and opportunities. Students with special needs did not receive the appropriate education they deserved until the middle of the twentieth century. Only in the last three decades with passage of the special education laws have services to students with special needs become available. Special educators are advocates for children with special needs and should not get caught in the politics that interfere with providing the needed special educational services for children with disabilities.

Intolerance Promotes a Cycle of Hostility

Intolerance in the long run perpetuates hostility—and causes victimization and immense harm. The attitude of intolerance creates a divide between "us" and "them" and leads to negativity that further leads to frustration and aggression. Aggression builds up when one side appears stronger and interferes with a natural desire for homogeneity. If the other side submits or agrees, tension diminishes, and if the other side desires to get even by inflicting harm, hostility develops. By addressing and acknowledging differences, one can prevent misunderstandings that have the potential for raising hostility.

In special education the relationship between suspension/expulsion and dropping out has become explicit. When the student is suspended due to a minor infraction of behavior, a message is transmitted to the student that he or she is not allowed to attend the school. Over time, however, he or she accepts the rejection by the school and becomes comfortable with the school's decision and begins to share dislike for school and education and then drops out. Clearly, intolerance of student disruptive behavior by the school results in student hostility toward learning. Tolerance for such minor infractions may at least keep the student in the classroom and with the increased opportunities for teaching and positive behavior supports; the student may turn around and become a good citizen of the school. Establishing behavior management systems that focus on preventive strategies and teaching of alternative responses, such as social skills, problem solving, and self-control, are likely to generate better outcomes for students than suspension.

WHY EDUCATORS NEED TO HAVE TOLERANCE

Schools represent society, and society represents many societal differences. Educators must accept and respect children of all origins, heritage, and appearances. They must not intentionally engage in discussions to damage religious beliefs or cultural behaviors or structures that provide a basis of identity and meaning to people. They must be open to differences in learning styles and behaviors and be cautious about their biases toward only accepting Caucasian behaviors as appropriate and punishing culturally different behaviors.

Special educators in particular, since they deal with learning and behavioral differences in children on a daily basis, are well aware of the long-term negative outcomes of intolerance. That is why they react to and reject zero tolerance toward disruptive behavior policies because they can foresee how tolerating an occurrence of disruptive behavior may be a better option for a student who is trying to work on her or his behavior at this time than expelling the student for a minor infraction. They know that teaching requires patience, and patience comes with tolerance for mistakes and errors.

Tolerance Does Not Mean Lack of Standards

Sometimes special educators get a bad rap for *tolerance*. They are viewed as having no or low standards for student learning or behavior and are often told by their administrators that special educators need "too much" to do "too little" with students with special needs. Instead of submitting to such criticisms, they must emphasize fairness and objective decision making that is intended to bring about improvements in student outcomes and behavior. While not all children with disabilities will be able to learn in the general education environment, no child should be excluded from education altogether. By creating an array of possible alternative learning environments for students who are unable to learn in typical classroom settings, they are able to meet the needs of many students.

The use of evidence-based practices for teaching academics and social behavior promotes engagement and prevents escalation of problem behavior. Special educators should show a thorough understanding of how to design and plan for instruction for children with special needs in various environments to keep them engaged in learning. By continually reviewing and critiquing their own impact and effectiveness, they should attempt to provide opportunities to children who show limited academic, social, or interpersonal skills to learn and practice these skills. They should maintain expectations that are conducive to producing positive social and academic outcomes for students with disabilities.

What Are the Soft Signs of Intolerance?

Intolerance develops when we fail to challenge our views and deny the other side. It is extremely important to periodically examine the other side of the issue. When faced with challenges, we go to our own comfort zone in thinking. From time to time, special educators take a moment, sit back, and reflect about how and why other professionals view them differently. For example, the next-door general educator, Marcy, has thirty-four students in her classroom, and when she notices Sally only has ten, she begins to compare her work with Sally's. She has limited knowledge about what it means to be a special educator, but she looks at the surface-level factors—a low teacher-student ratio, assistance from paraprofessionals, and student helpers. Marcy has started making negative comments and has engaged in teasing and sometimes indirect ridicule or insult. For example, Sally hears from Marcy, "I wonder what you do in special education." "You have two paraprofessionals in your classroom, you don't even have to teach ... Gee. How much help do you need? All I see you do is just sit behind the table and work with small groups of kids." "Your students don't have to take the state tests."

Special educators must not let such behaviors intimidate and degrade them. They may like to invite the general educators and other professionals to their classrooms and show them their work and help them understand the nature of their work by providing them an opportunity for professional learning. They must not let constant nagging, workload, or greater numbers humiliate them or deprive them of their status as a special education teacher.

RECOMMENDATIONS

Special educators face formidable challenges. Tolerance guides them toward improvement in their entire life; it makes them a better teacher, a better behavior manager, and a better leader. They establish a clear purpose for student learning, keeping in mind both academic and social outcomes for students with disabilities and reflecting on what they can really tolerate and what is completely intolerable.

They keep their focus on how to work with each student and enable them to achieve their educational goals. For each expectation, they assess where their students are and what they need to learn, and they provide them with clear and specific behavioral examples of positive behaviors. They teach and review expectations throughout the school year. When students engage in positive desired behavior, special educators notice and attend to positive behavior and encourage them for being positive, on-task, and appropriate.

Teach Students Their Limits

Children, including those with disabilities, need limits. They need to know what the rules are and what happens when rules are not followed. They also need help with following the rules. Special educators know they may have to prompt some of their students more than others or physically guide the ones who have physical and cognitive delays so they are able to follow the rules. Some students with special needs poorly respond to unclear rules, or rigid or inconsistent enforcement of rules. By using a balance between firmness and flexibility, special educators help get their students closer to their educational goals.

Provide Multiple Opportunities

Special educators provide their students with multiple opportunities to learn a behavior and provide specific feedback for appropriate behavior. They teach them the necessary social skills that may enhance their overall social functioning in the classroom and in the school.

When dealing with students who have histories of school-based behavior problems, they develop procedures for discouraging problem behavior and review and revise current discipline policies to provide clear definitions of disruptive behavior and minor infractions. Also, feedback on a minor infraction is provided, and students are taught to take control of his or her behavior to prevent further occurrences of such behavior leading them to the principal's office. Students need feedback on what not to do, when not to behave a certain way. Special educators know which behaviors should be managed in the classroom and which behaviors force the student to be sent to the office or to a quiet supervised area.

Data-based Decision Making

Special educators develop data-based decision rules to ensure that appropriate strategies are used with students who frequently receive administrative action as a result of problem behavior. They keep track of behavioral issues in their classroom and reflect upon whether they need to change their teaching or management strategies. They attempt to explore alternatives when they notice that a student is removed from the classroom three times for the same problem behavior. Also, they recommend a team-based approach to develop alternatives, such as more effective management and discipline strategies for the student not responding to a specific intervention.

In addition, they develop procedures for record-keeping and documentation. Using multiple sources of data including surveys, anecdotal information, student evaluations, parent reports, office referrals, and discipline reports, they make informed decisions about the overall effectiveness of their behavior management system and are willing to refine it. They work closely with parents and families and encourage them to participate in the development of IEPs, transition plans, and behavioral intervention plans. To ensure that their classroom system responds to the cultural, language, and ethnic makeup of the community in which the school resides, special educators must work with the community. Each child is different and responds to the same system differently, and a fairly homogeneous education is impossible and undesirable.

SUMMARY

Tolerance is one of the most needed attributes of a special educator. Although many special educators show a tendency or an inclination to be tolerant, it is a quality that can be taught and bolstered with training and experience. Special educators embrace tolerance because it keeps them focused on student outcomes and keeps them from blaming the child when things do not go the desired way.

Tolerance enhances the capacity of the special educator not only in instructional decision making but also in maintaining personal connections and professional transactions. Going back to Mary's example, when Mary is outside of her work setting, she demonstrates tolerance toward her family members and peers. With her seven-year-old boy, she shows tolerance by listening to him without judging him. Her son has an issue with his friendship skills, he gets upset with them, and he does not want to go out to play with them. She does not say "you should stop talking to him" or "you need to find another friend." In listening to his concerns, she does not always agree with him, does not put his friends down or belittle them, but uses active listening and opportunity learning to teach him how to have healthy relationships with peers. She also teaches him flexibility by sharing with him the importance of how in relationships sometimes he needs to give in and sometimes he needs to compromise to keep the relationships. At the same time, he needs to make his concerns known to his friend and he needs to weigh in the common good for himself and his peers.

With her neighbors and peers, she is known to be approachable. She makes time for them. In her neighborhood, she works with a parent group and assists them in providing information on evidence-based special education services that have benefitted many children with special needs. In her personal and professional life, she finds time to listen to concerns of others, tries to be unbiased, and when someone asks for advice, she gathers information from various perspectives. In her personal or professional interactions, she is not tolerant toward devaluing the special education profession and does not allow others to destroy the profession's image.

REFERENCE

The American heritage dictionary of the English language. 4th ed. 2000.

Chapter Three

Empathy and Active Listening

Sheila has been teaching middle school students with emotional/behavioral disorders for twenty years. She learned early in her career that when her students acted out or withdrew they were communicating to her; it was her job to figure out what they were trying to communicate. She learned also to recognize the early warning signs of her students' frustration. She found that by being able to recognize her students' warning signs that she could prevent many behavior problems. Students respected Sheila because she was fair to them and she always listened to what they were saying to her. One of her students later went to college and wrote to Sheila, saying: "Thank you for always caring and listening to what I had to say. You understood me when no one else did. I am where I am today because you cared about me and treated me like a real person."

Now Sheila is trying to care for her mother. Her mother still lives in her own home, but Sheila needs to check in on her every evening. Sheila's own children are now grown, and her husband helps her with her mother's care as well. Sheila is finding that her mother really looks forward to Sheila's evening visits and wants to hear all about her day. When Sheila says it is time for her to get home, Sheila's mother begins complaining about her aches and pains and how she has been kind of down that day and she just doesn't have much to do and never has any company. Sheila has learned to actively listen to what her mother is saying. She knows that she needs to empathize with her mother. She works hard not to deny her mother's feelings—instead, she asks questions to help her better understand what her mother is saying to her. She has figured out that her mother doesn't want her to leave—her mother wants her company and behaves by complaining about aches and pains in an effort to get Sheila to stay at her house longer. She is hearing her mother say that she needs more to keep her busy.

Sheila decides that she will ask her mother if she would be willing to help her make some items for her classroom. Sheila really needs some chair covers for her class and needs some additional decorations, and her mother is an excellent seamstress. One night she tells her mother that she could really use her help in making the chair covers and some other things for her class. Her mother is very excited about the idea and gets to work on the project right away. When Sheila comes in the evening, her mother is eager to show her what she has done and soon doesn't care if Sheila stays long because she wants to get back to her project. When some other teachers see what Sheila's mother has done, they ask for her mother's help. Soon some of the other teachers are coming over to Sheila's mother's house to see her. Sheila worked to put herself in the place of her students and her mother, and by listening to them and recognizing their needs, she was successful in both settings.

The special educator shows that he or she has adopted what Wood and Long (1991) call the "ethics of helping" (p. 158). If we are to help our students, we must engage in supportive actions that show our students we care and are genuinely interested in helping them when they need us. Sheila exhibited the ethics of helping both within her classroom and with her mother. Because Sheila learned how important it was that she engage in helping her students, it became a habit for her throughout her lifetime. She engaged in active listening and is an empathetic individual.

In today's society, adults continually complain in the workplace that their coworkers and their bosses don't listen to them. They complain that nobody seems to understand what they are going through. Communication can easily break down in the workplace. Frustration sets in, and people either leave or are asked to leave their jobs.

Through working in the field of special education, Sheila has learned how to prevent a communication breakdown. What were the specific skills that she learned to use throughout her life?

ACTIVE LISTENING

We live in a rushed society, and oftentimes we don't always take the time to attend to our students and listen to what they are really saying to us. Because we are not paying attention to them—we are thinking about what we have to get done after school, what we are going to do over the weekend, that IEP that is coming up shortly, the parent conference that we need to get done—our children know this and they perceive that we are just too busy to really care about them. We have all gotten so used to doing two things at one time that we may find ourselves trying to do that when children really need our undivided attention.

Most of us are cognizant of whether a colleague or family member is listening to us. That individual may pretend to be listening but is looking at his emails or glancing at the newspaper. The message that the individual is sending to us is that he has other things to do and doesn't care to be bothered. We usually quit talking to the person—in many cases we are insulted that he isn't interested in what we have to say. We must be very careful that we are not conveying such a message to our students.

Our students with special needs are precious individuals who need to know that we will attend to their needs. Good special educators have learned the importance of actively listening to their students. When the student is struggling with a math problem or completing an assignment, the special educator goes to the student and listens to what the student is saying about what he or she is experiencing. The special educator looks at the student, blocks out all distractions, and gives the student the needed attention. He or she is cognizant of the voice tone, the body language, and the message underlying what the student is actually saying.

Schrumpf, Crawford, and Bodine (1991) define *active listening* as "the ability to use nonverbal behaviors to exhibit that you hear and understand." Nonverbal behaviors can include: tone of voice, eye contact, facial expressions, posture, and gestures. If you are leaning forward, smiling, nodding your head, and ignoring outside distractions, you are actively listening" (p. 17).

Active listening is a lifelong skill that serves the special educator well in all arenas. When the special educator is supporting an aging or sick parent, the special educator gives the parent the undivided attention that is needed and listens to the real meaning behind the actual words. When we are talking to a friend or colleague and they are sharing a concern, we give them our undivided attention so they know that we care enough about them to stop whatever else we are doing and devote our precious time to only them.

Recognizing Frustration

Special educators recognize the frustration cycle—the steps that are seen when students are becoming upset and are in need of assistance from the special educator. Good special educators look for those signs of frustration—the tapping of the pencil, the facial frown, the hidden verbal messages—and they intervene at the first signs of frustration to prevent the student from becoming very upset. They learn to "read" their students. They really get to know them and know what might be difficult for them.

They engage in preventive solutions—they use proximity control, they provide supportive assistance when the student is struggling ("How can I help you with that math problem?"). They have learned to move more closely to the student—not getting in the student's face but being near the student to see what they can do to help. They are not confrontational—they are supportive.

They provide hurdle help to the child—"looks like you are having trouble with number 3, how about if you go on to the next two questions and then I will come back and help you with number 3?" It is sometimes difficult for students with special needs to recognize that if you can't succeed in a particular task, you need to go on and strive to do what you can. They think that if they get to problem #3 and can't do it then it is the end of the line and they have failed when, in fact, there might just be one problem they can't do and the remainder of the problems they could solve.

Special educators use "antiseptic bouncing." They recognize when a student is struggling with a task and offer a different activity for the student or a break from the task. Statements such as: "How about if you go sharpen your pencil and then come back and work on this paper?" or "I have an errand I need you to do for me. Will you take this to the office?"

Such skills serve individuals throughout their lives. We have learned from these techniques that they assist us in getting a particular job done. When we are getting frustrated with doing a difficult task, we take a short break or we leave a task behind temporarily and move on to the next item we need to do. We have also learned to provide supportive assistance to individuals who are frustrated with specific tasks they are asked to do.

We might be taking a knitting class or an Excel class with a friend and because we have learned to see the signs of frustration, we will offer assistance to our friend so that he or she can successfully complete the task.

Recognizing Feelings

The special educator has learned the importance of recognizing the feelings of his or her students. If the student responds by saying that something is "too hard or "I just don't know how to do this," the immediate reaction from the teacher could be to deny the student's feelings by quickly responding: "Oh, now, you know that is really easy" or "Sure, you know how to do that." Such a denial of what the student is saying will frustrate the child even more. The teacher hasn't truly listened to the student. The student is crying for help and needs the teacher's assistance. The special educator should be fact-finding with supportive comments. The supportive special educator says: "Can you tell me how I can help you with that?" or "What is giving you the most difficulty?" These statements recognize that the student is having difficulty.

One of the authors remembers an incident many years ago when a child blurted out to her in frustration: "I don't like Mrs. Stallings." Because Mrs. Stallings was a wonderful teacher, the author remembers replying: "Now you know we all like Mrs. Stallings." The student then proceeded to throw a temper tantrum. That tantrum could have easily been avoided if the author would have said: "Can you tell me what is bothering you about Mrs. Stallings?" or "Sounds like you are very upset right now, do you want to talk about it?"

Special educators have learned the importance of recognizing the feelings of the student and listening to the message behind the words. In everyday life we may catch ourselves refusing to acknowledge our colleagues' or family members' feelings. In Sheila's case, it would have been so easy when her mother complained about her aches and pains for Sheila to respond: "Oh, Mother, there is nothing wrong with you," but Sheila knew from her many years in special education the importance of recognizing her mother's feelings and being supportive.

Many of us have probably experienced the loss of a loved one and someone comes to the funeral home or memorial service to offer his/her condolences. The individual may make a statement like: "Oh, you are lucky she didn't suffer long." If you have lost a loved one, you don't want someone to downplay your grief. You want individuals who will recognize your grief and give you their condolences: "I am so sorry to hear about your mother; you have my sympathy."

Behavior Is Communication

Sheila was experienced in recognizing a key lesson—when someone is behaving in a certain way they are communicating with us, and good special educators become good detectives. They learn to figure out why the student is doing what he or she is doing. Every behavior has a function—it may be access to attention or power and control; it may be escape or avoidance from a task that is perceived as too difficult or not desirable or the student doesn't want to perform the task in front of peers; or it may be designed to meet a sensory need for movement or for visual, auditory, oral, or tactile satisfaction.

This is functional assessment—figuring out what need the student has that results in the student communicating through his or her own behavior.

The good special educator is continually assessing the function of the student's behavior—what function does this particular behavior serve for the student? The student is the class clown—he is in need of attention. Rather than getting attention from being the class clown, the special educator may want to see that the student gets his need for attention met by serving as a class leader on a specific project in which the student excels.

If the student is engaging in avoidance behavior on a task, then the special educator looks closely at the task to determine why the student perceives it in a negative way. Perhaps the student is bothered because there is too much on a page. The teacher can then break the task down over several pages so the student doesn't need to see the whole assignment at one time. Some students with sensitivity to certain senses might be bothered by loud noises or bright lights. The teacher can work to avoid those particular situations within the classroom. The teacher will want to make sure that the student is not seated right under a bright or fluorescent light.

The ability to see the function of behavior is a critical skill in life. We have to deal with the behavior of those individuals in the service industry, the behaviors of our colleagues and our bosses, the behaviors of our family members, and the behaviors of other people we encounter in our everyday life. If we understand the basic concept that behavior is communication and that all behavior serves a purpose, we can work to change the behavior of individuals in a positive manner.

We may become frustrated with a boss who will not allow anything to be done unless he or she specifically approves it. That individual needs access to power and control and needs to be involved in decision making. That individual is afraid of losing control, and until we recognize that, we cannot effectively work with the individual. Instead, we must learn to inform that individual of any decisions that need to be made.

Separating the Words Being Said from the Person

Special educators develop thick skin in their work. Sheila learned early on that her students would deliberately say hurtful things to her because they were hurting themselves. She again learned to recognize their messages and didn't take their comments personally. The special educator does not allow the student to use words to hurt him or her. The special educator directs the student back to what needs to be done.

Some students have learned that calling the teacher a name like "fatty" or "thunder thighs" or "four-eyed bi ..." may offend the teacher and will hurt and, in fact, divert the attention of the teacher to the name called rather than what is being expected of the student. The effective special educator will ignore the comment—being very careful that he or she does not exude the appearance that the name bothers him or her. It may hurt the teacher inside, but he or she must be very careful not to let the student know that. If the student believes that when he calls the teacher "fatty" that it bothers her, he will continue to use the name-calling to get to the teacher and divert the attention away from what is being expected of the student.

If the student learns that he or she cannot manipulate the teacher by calling him or her names, he may then try to call family members of the teacher names. Again, the student is trying to find the magic words that will hurt the teacher and get the teacher off the track of the student expectations.

If calling the teacher's family members names doesn't seem to bother the teacher, then what the student may do is to attack the values of the teacher. "You are the worst teacher I have ever had" or "You are prejudiced." This really bothers many teachers because they don't want to be perceived as a bad teacher or as being prejudiced. Again, the special educator does not allow the student to get off track and sticks to the issue at hand. Children like to manipulate and can't be allowed to do so. The teacher will, however, want to determine why the student is attacking the teacher—what is he or she really angry about?

In life, we may become angry with friends or family at something that one of them said. Special educators have learned that it is critical to separate the words from the person. At times we all make comments that we wish we would not have made or we do things that unfortunately we cannot undo. However, the positive special educator will not let that harm his beliefs in the person. How many times have we heard: "I like you but right now I don't like your behavior."

EMPATHY

Good teachers are empathetic individuals. They attempt to put themselves in the place of the student and understand what the student is experiencing. We are all reminded of the former president of the United States, who would appear on television and say: "I feel your pain." He probably didn't "feel the pain" of many Americans, but he said it in a way that convinced everyone he did.

A commentator on TV during the recent presidential election discussed the importance of this empathy as being a critical component in how people decide for whom they will vote. Individuals who are empathetic display an intuitive sense of what another person is facing.

Granted, we have not experienced some of the pain that our students may have experienced—abuse, homelessness, fear of being shot in the neighborhood—but good special educators can make those supportive statements to the students that convey that they understand that the student is upset and they are concerned when the student is concerned and they are working hard to understand the feelings that the child is having. The special educator is compassionate and caring, and the child believes that the special educator is feeling their pain.

Lavoie (2005) has defined empathy as "the ability to view a situation from another person's point of view" (p. 238). He advocates the importance of teaching our students how to be empathetic by outlining our emotional reaction to their behavior or comments. That way the child becomes aware of the impact of their behavior on others. Good special educators work with their students to let them know the impact their behavior has on others. They do this through role-playing, through private conversations with the student when the student is not upset, and, of course, by modeling appropriate behavior at all times.

Empathy is a difficult skill for students who have social skills problems to learn, so it is critical that we model empathy with our students (Walker, Colvin, and Ramsey, 1995).

Effective special educators must first understand that their behavior has a serious impact on their students. They know that the words they use with children must be supportive, not mean or hateful. They learn that their students pay close attention to what the teachers say to them. We all can remember teachers who said either supportive or nonsupportive statements to us, and some of those comments we have never forgotten.

The author has always remembered a teacher who told her that her artwork was "trite." The author had worked very hard on her artwork and was devastated by such a comment. That teacher was not empathetic, and if she could have viewed the situation from the author's point of view, she would have never said such a hurtful and derogatory comment.

Some teachers might say that the student is lazy because the student is lethargic. A student with special needs may be worn out because he or she has had to spend a great deal of time on a task that was very difficult. It isn't that the student is lazy—instead, the student is legitimately tired from working on a difficult task. Imagine how all of us feel when we have finished a task that was difficult for us. We are worn out and are ready to rest. We aren't lazy—we are just "wiped out."

Wood and Long (1991) relate that when a student is in a crisis the adult must "have a genuine desire to help the student rather than to express personal reactions to the incident" (p. 158). The empathetic special educator is quick to not judge the student but to try to view the situation the way the student is seeing it. This sometimes is easier said than done because we may want to impose our own values on them and give them a solution that would work for us. However, given that child's circumstances, our own value system will probably not work for the student.

Wood and Long (1991) believe that the adult must first recognize the feelings and the anxieties that are expressed in the student's behavior. They must then convey this understanding to the student and then will need to eventually teach their students how to recognize their own feelings.

CONFLICT RESOLUTION

Conflict is an everyday reality. We run into conflict at work, at home, at the grocery store, and in many other settings. We can choose to avoid conflict, to become argumentative, or to communicate to try to resolve the conflict. Because active listening and empathy are keys to the success of conflict resolution skills, special educators have learned to resolve conflict in a peaceful manner. They have learned how to communicate effectively to resolve conflict.

When two students are in conflict with each other, the special educator brings them together and models active listening and empathy. He or she remains neutral and listens to both sides and teaches her students to do the same. Each student gets a chance to tell his or her side of the story. The teacher then clarifies issues and encourages the students to brainstorm possible win-win solutions to their problems.

When the special educator models such conflict resolution, he or she is teaching the student a lifelong skill because the special educator knows how often those skills are applied in real life. Individuals must learn to effectively communicate with others who may not see things the way they see things.

Conflict resolution skills are important life skills. Special educators use those conflict resolution skills in life with their family members and friends. They are constantly looking for common ground to solve problems. They have learned how to communicate effectively to express their own needs and to actively listen to the needs of others. They try to find peaceful solutions to problems.

They find themselves mediating conflicts, trying to get people to resolve their differences rather than to continue to argue and fight. They have learned that failure to resolve conflict peacefully may cause lifetime grudges that eat away at individuals and cause them to be dissatisfied throughout life. They find themselves problem solving in the grocery store when the checker wants to argue with them, at the gas station when someone is arguing that they were waiting in line first, and within the school when a colleague argues that her way of teaching is the only way to teach.

Letting a Problem Go

The special educator learns quickly to let a problem go once the issue has been resolved. There is no place in special education for holding a grudge against the student. Once an issue is over, it should be over and dropped. When a student has gotten into trouble and needs to receive a consequence for the problem exhibited and needs to be talked to about the problem, the consequence is rendered and then life goes on.

The special educator should always have the attitude that tomorrow is another day and the incident is forgotten and not brought up again the next day. The special educator models that for her other students so they learn the value of resolving a problem and not holding a grudge. When a student has had a crisis and the consequence is rendered and the discussion about it is over, the special educator will leave the student with a vote of confidence. He or she might say: "I know you can have a good rest of the day." This shows the student that the special educator has confidence that he or she can turn his or her day around.

The special educator weighs his or her words carefully so that he or she doesn't say anything that will be regretted later. He or she has learned to think before talking and acting. The special educator models control and calmness in dealing with all problems. The special educator also models forgiveness.

This is an important life skill because the authors can guarantee hearing of individuals who still don't speak to other individuals because of something that happened twenty-five years ago. Special educators learn to let it go and to work to resolve the issues that are causing a rift. If the special educator has a conflict with a family member, the special educator works with the individual to resolve the difference amicably and then stresses that the incident is over and it is forgotten.

SUMMARY

When working with students with special needs, the competent special educator has learned the important skills of actively listening to what the student is saying and doing. The special educator is not confrontational; he or she is supportive and genuinely listens to what the student is trying to communicate through his words or behavior.

While engaging in active listening, the special educator exhibits empathy—the ability to see the student's point of view. The special educator separates the words being said from the person. Conflict is resolved peacefully, and the student learns alternative skills for dealing with his or her anger through the modeling the student sees by the teacher.

The skills of active listening and empathy serve the special educator throughout life as conflicts arise.

REFERENCES

Lavoie, R. (2005). *It's so much work to be your friend.* New York: Touchstone Books.

Schrumpf, F., Crawford, D., and Bodine, R. (1991). *Peer mediation: Conflict resolution in schools. Student manual.* Champaign, Illinois: Research Press.

Walker, H., Colvin, G., and Ramsey, E. (1995). *Antisocial behavior in school: Strategies and best practices.* Pacific Grove, California: Brooks/Cole.

Wood, M., and Long, N. (1991). *Life space intervention: Talking with children and youth in crisis.* Austin, Texas: Pro-Ed.

Chapter Four

The Ability to Build
Relationships with Students

It was the evening before the first day of school. Andrea felt both the thrill that comes from a positively anticipated venture and the excitement that connects to anxious feelings when embarking into the unknown. Many questions went through her mind about her new special education students. She looked forward to developing solid rapport and honest relationships with them.

One of the more experienced teachers at her new school had advised her not to crack a smile for a month so the students would know she was in charge. To her that seemed unnatural. On the other hand, she did not want to present herself as a pushover, concerned that students would gain the upper hand and pick up on her inexperience. She knew she would have to find the balance, and hopefully her training and instincts would serve her well on day one.

FORMING THE TEACHER/STUDENT RELATIONSHIP

So much goes into any human relationship, whether with family, friends, coworkers, or students. True professionals are able to make the distinction between each and at the same time be authentic with everyone they encounter. To do so takes maturity and judgment, care and confidence. Following are seven suggestions for Andrea and all special educators so that connections with students begin successfully and remain positive through the time that the student and teacher work together.

1. Notice the student. To truly notice a student, a teacher has to approach the student in the teacher's role as a caring human being and also as a professional assessing the strengths and needs of the student. When encountering a student, a teacher has all antennae out. This means consciously taking in all aspects of the student from head to foot.

When starting from top to toe, note the facial expression. Does the student appear alert? What is the student's mood? Does the facial expression indicate a sense of confidence or wariness? Does the student offer eye contact, or are the eyes downcast? Does the student use a soft or audible voice? Does the tone of voice indicate anything about the student? Does the student's dress send any signals that distinguish him or her from the others? Do styles, colors, accessories, or condition of the garments tell you anything? What objects does the student carry or keep on hand that signal unstated aspects of the personality?

When in an academic situation, does the student appear comfortable and confident or restless, unfocused, and apprehensive? How does the student respond to others in the classroom? When and with whom is the student most comfortable?

2. Listen to the student. When a student speaks, listen with the ears and also listen with intuition. Sometimes students will speak in a straightforward manner, and the teacher knows exactly what the young person means. At other times the student will be cryptic, and the teacher must read between the lines. Experience with how a student typically acts will offer a baseline to distinguish notable changes. From there the teacher is able to determine if a student is sending a distress signal or using manipulative behavior. A teacher not only must listen to audible sounds but also must have an ear to the ground by noting what might be behind voice tone and unclear communications.

3. Pay attention to your feelings and instincts when with the student or when thinking about the student. A teacher may experience a range of emotions and questions when in the presence of any student. Because a special educator has a more intensive relationship with a student, the opportunity to develop the "inner eyes and ears" presents itself.

A teacher tapping into intuition knows that something is happening that needs further exploration when the inner bells go off. A teacher may feel a sense of discomfort, uneasiness, or unrest around a student. Sometimes a highly intuitive teacher can even tap into the student's emotions by feeling a sense of sadness or fear along with the child. When this occurs the teacher must work to differentiate between personal feelings before exploring what the student may be feeling at the time.

School days are packed with many interactions and impressions. It is impossible to process every important impression and address it immediately. When a teacher takes an after-school walk or reviews the day right before dropping off to sleep, something may come to mind that is worthy of note. At that time a teacher can review an event or impression and determine what would be the best response. Maybe the sense the teacher has about the student will lead to further review or be the final piece of an ongoing puzzle that will help lead the teacher in determining how best to approach a circumstance.

4. Be present with each student. When someone is fully present with us, we know it because we see that the person is giving us eye contact, responding to what we say, pacing each reply so that we are properly heard, and acting as if no one else matters at this moment but us. The facial expressions match the content of the conversation and enhance the sense of safety. Thus, we feel encouraged to continue with the interaction. When a teacher presents to a student in this way, he or she sends the signal that the student is significant and that the matter of the moment counts.

A teacher who is able to be present also knows when to pause or to even refrain from initiating conversation. This teacher knows when the child feels safe enough to share or if the student is not ready to go further in revealing a matter of importance. A teacher with cultivated sensitivity to students knows what would be funny for the child, what kind of jesting would be appropriate teasing.

5. Show the student respect. A teacher can be confident in the role of a professional and, from the position of self-respect, offer likewise to the student. Bringing awareness of past and current events in the life of the student and knowing the young person's social and emotional history, the teacher faces the student to present an assignment, to send them to the nurse for a medication, or to review a math problem.

Treating the student with respect brings to bear acting appropriately in the mutual space created with the student. This could include voice volume, positioning oneself at eye level, and speaking with purpose and personality. Sensitivity to what physical touch a student tolerates is important. Some students, due to their disability area, respond negatively to touch. Others crave attention and appreciate a hand on the shoulder, a high five, or a tap on the finger.

A respectful teacher knows why students are saying what they are saying, balancing spontaneous exchanges with strategic messages. Familiarity and common sense weigh in, enabling the teacher to create meaningful, personalized, and effective communication with students.

6. Reinforce and discourage behaviors as appropriate. Some students respond positively to a look, a touch, a well-tailored and timed phrase. Others react negatively to a poorly chosen reaction by a teacher that could then create a greater chasm between them. Interaction with students with special needs can be delicate at times. Thus it is important that the teacher be aware of the range of responses that a student is capable of making, while also being attuned to the child's personal behaviors, moods, and internal reactions.

A self-possessed teacher can lend stability to the emotional and social climate of the classroom and to the emotional and social reality of a student. Once a teacher has internalized academic, social, and emotional knowledge of a student, he or she increases the likelihood of optimal conversational choices with individual students. In doing so a teacher supports the student and helps maintain open and workable communication lines with a student. As communication grows in a positive direction, the teacher/student relationship becomes more solid, natural, and comfortable.

When inappropriate behavior does occur, the teacher needs to be consistent and effective in handling it. In time and with awareness, teachers learn to apply building, program, and individual behavioral plans as specified by the IEP. Balancing general guidelines with strategies particular to the student is an art and skill unique to the teacher's personality, professional development level, and experience.

7. Show acceptance through ups and downs. When a behavioral incident occurs, the steady relational connection that had been established between student and teacher can disintegrate. When the student receives a consequence for an inappropriate behavior, she may show hesitation about reconnecting to the arbiter of the consequence out of discomfort, fear, or shame. Thus it is up to the teacher to seek out the student and show by word and action that the student is still viewed with acceptance and care. By using familiar phrases, acting "normal," and resuming the ordinary, the teacher offers the student solid ground upon which to move forward.

As the mature adult, the teacher then assures the student that it is possible to make a fresh start. The teacher who helps the student separate the person from the action assumes the role of assisting the student back to comfort and emotional balance. Explaining to the student why the action was unacceptable and offering alternative behavioral options for the future gives the student a sense of security and direction. When a teacher tells the student that it is possible to slip up, that the behavior could even happen again and that there are ways to improve, the student and the teacher can reunite to work together to restore balance within the student and in the classroom community as well.

MAINTAINING HEALTHY BOUNDARIES WITH STUDENTS

Through the ins and outs of relating with a student, a key challenge for staff is to maintain appropriate boundaries. In and through offering supportive conversation and academic information, a teacher must remain self-possessed. In this situation, that means centered in one's own life and being, knowing where one's emotional and social life ends and where that of the child begins.

Teachers who know themselves well fulfill their needs outside the school setting. They come to work with a "full cup" in order to enter into the give-and-take of school life without any unconscious expectations that the love and admiration of students will fulfill any needs for recognition and care. Thus, as whole persons, aware of their emotional ranges and sentiments, teachers then relate with students with emotional honesty and evenness. When at school, these teachers are all about school. When at home or in other situations, these teachers maintain presence primarily with those who are part of those aspects of life as well.

A teacher needs to be aware of how personal emotions connect to life events, past and present. When in school, a teacher works best when able to seal off personal issues of anger and resentment, fear, shame, and insecurity. When at school, a teacher has to be aware of what sets them off and be able to sift that out from what happens when engaged in interaction with a student.

Wherever the teacher is, it is important to blend together authenticity and appropriateness as fits the circumstances. A teacher has to know what aspects of personhood to put forth and which to withhold. A teacher must be sensitive to the moment, whether "on" in the school environment or in downtimes with family and friends. That way, boundaries fit the people and places. If home base is firmly established within the mind, heart, and emotions of the teacher, any shifts among persons and places should come as second nature. The teacher will automatically make comments and act from a place of appropriate interest and care rather than from an unresolved past issue or unaddressed personal concern.

SHOWING INTEREST AND CARE

Some students are easier to work with, be around, and just plain easier to like than others. Yet, being professionals, teachers manage to mete out just the right levels of care fitting for each child, their needs and the academic setting. They assess the situation and, based on perspective and experience, decide when a student needs sincere affirmation or when a compliment would interfere with a child's direction with a project and even be a distraction.

Care begins with interest and develops over time. Common projects in common environments set the stage for care. Teachers show up consistently and decide to attend not only to academics but also to students as persons. Thus, optimal conditions exist for teachers who remain alert to many factors and show interest in the actions, needs, and possibilities of their students.

Approaching students with lines of questioning that begin at their comfort level and lead to the safe expression of their struggles and of their dreams supports a successful relationship. Perhaps a child harbors a fear or a doubt. When a teacher opens the door to sharing by laying the firm ground of security and trust, a child receives validation. When a teacher sets the stage for a child to risk expressing their future goals to an adult who believes in their possibilities, they increase the likelihood that their dreams will become realized in the future.

Supporting students in the individual expressions of their uncertainties brings them to the ability to take small steps through and past the barriers that impede confident strides toward exciting possibilities. Sometimes all it takes is a simple reply to a risked sharing from a student to encourage the child to say more and more. A mere "really," "wow," "hmmm," or "yes" enables a student to come forward with the whole picture.

This whole picture could be the description of an abusive situation from which a teacher's response can be the first step of rescue. The whole picture can also be the explanation of the interest to train to be a mechanic or a nurse or an actor. The teacher, serving as a mirror, can speak back to the young person the assurance that the talent and resolve lies within them to do it.

Both the teacher and the student bring pieces of possibility to their exchanges. A wise and astute teacher is able to artfully listen, provide affirmation, and assist a student in describing reality and projecting potential success and fulfillment into the future.

INTERPRETING STUDENT BEHAVIOR

When one student grimaces, it may mean something completely different than when another makes the same expression. Perhaps one student experienced a physical discomfort from digesting lunch, while the other thought of the threat of being punched if he did not keep a sibling's secret.

When one student sheds a tear it may have been caused by allergies while with another, it could connect to a recent loss such as the death of a beloved pet. When one student frowns when looking at numbers on the board, it may be the indication of the beginning of visual problems. It shows that a child needs an eye exam. When another frowns when looking at the same numbers it may be due to the fact that he does not understand the problem.

Students present with many and varied facial expressions that challenge the teacher for interpretation. The teacher then needs to sort out facts in order to determine how to read any clues provided by facial expressions. Does the expression connect to a current or potential health problem? Does it connect to emotions of fear or anxiety? Do any new events in the student's life connect to the expression? Does the student understand the academic material? Does the teacher need to provide more background information for the student? Does the teacher need to add further visual, auditory, tactile, or kinesthetic dimensions to the lesson so the student will be better able to access the information?

When a student speaks to staff or peers, does he directly disclose what he means or does he speak in a veiled manner, requiring the adult to ask questions or make interpretations? Does speech reveal clarity or require a speech screening? Does content contain correct grammar, or does the child need assistance with proper use of the language? Is the student sharing in a comfortable conversational style, or does speaking with adults generally cause uneasiness? Is the student putting out a small portion of an area of concern, testing the waters to see if the adult can be trusted with more? Teachers engaged in dialogue with students often face the complex task of discerning the child's needs, content, and exact message.

When special education teachers observe students engaged in social play during downtime or teamed to work on a cooperative project, their natural antennae join with their heightened vigilance and trained "gut" to catch the common and sort out the significant. Being veterans of many academic tests, social interviews, social skills groups, and behavioral observations, their trained eyes and ears continuously assimilate data.

This data offers a backdrop for the discovery of academic deficits and strengths. This information points to qualifying scores for service or scores that indicate success and potential discontinuance of service. Special educators conducting formal interviews, social skills groups, and behavioral observations notice students' ability to relate in ways appropriate to age and circumstances. They also notice the lack of social skills that invite direct instruction to support and improve these skills.

Thus, trained and familiar with academic, social, and behavioral baselines, a special education professional does retain these skills when outside the testing situation. When special education teachers offer instruction, supervise in the lunchroom, team with classroom teachers, and work among a range of students, they continue to pick up on students' academic challenges, social difficulties, and emotional distress.

What teachers gather enables them to support and enhance formal data, offer input to parents during conferences or casual conversations, and provide informal insight to classroom teachers when they team in a collaborative setting. Special educators transform on-the-spot observations into spontaneous decisions in order to connect with students academically, socially, and emotionally.

Teachers who learn about the child's health through records or notice new responses have an edge because they can get to the issue faster and also know what questions to ask a parent or school nurse to better help the child. Teachers who understand multimodal teaching offer students more extensive access to information than those who operate simply in one dimension, such as lecturing. Teachers who listen for a child's message with an ear for the facts as well as the affective content learn the full meaning of what a student is saying.

These master communicators appear to engage with students very easily and naturally. Special educators, going about their daily work, provide full presence to support and relate with a range of students at varied academic levels and social/emotional places. Yet doing so is far from simple. When a teacher makes a small change in expression or switch in manner of content presentation, he or she evidences skilled professional training and innate ability.

USING THIS LIFE SKILL BEYOND THE CLASSROOM

We left the make-believe special educator, Andrea, introduced at the beginning of the chapter, wondering how she would fare in her relationships with students. Let us assume that she combined her training with her natural instincts and talents for working with students with special needs. Let us also assume that she incorporated into her interactions with young people the seven suggestions for making successful connections and enduring relationships with students. Let us revisit her, far beyond the first day of school.

Since she is working well with her students, we will view her life beyond the classroom twenty-five years hence. Let's look at Andrea with the belief that she, like all accomplished special educators, has integrated her relational skills when working with staff and when relating with family and friends.

When Andrea speaks with her peers and with parents, she gains their trust by speaking directly and clearly, using consistent eye contact. She speaks with clarity and consistency about all matters. She is direct, yet nonthreatening. She maintains integrity when speaking between individuals and interest groups. She bridges faculty factions by treating each with objectivity and honesty. Andrea finds support within her school district among other special educators who understand her world. Consequently, when in her setting, she knows which staff in that group to rely on to review her challenges. In addition, she is able to associate with staff members with objectivity, providing leadership as needed. Her perspective is clear because she is not seeking social approval from staff.

She chooses to find social support outside of the school community for personal matters. Thus, Andrea has no inclination to establish close friendships with those she may need to challenge or confront on behalf of a student. Andrea works in her school among a variety of adults. She greets everyone pleasantly, treats all respectfully, and remains singular yet part of the group. She attends functions, provides treats, makes the rounds at staff parties, yet she knows the line where her personal life begins. She is sociable but does not depend on the school social system for her entire social life.

Andrea keeps communication lines open with the parents of her students by various means. As appropriate, she uses a traveling notebook, the telephone, notes, formal letters, email, a newsletter, and conferences. She remains in touch on a continuous basis so parents experience no surprises. They respect her for being up-front with information and respond to her invitation to create a team on behalf of their child.

Andrea's life outside her workday includes time with her immediate family, other relatives, and friends. Do they know a different Andrea than the students, staff, and families know? The answer to this is "yes" and "no." Due to personal boundaries, she reveals parts of herself exclusively to those family and friends on her inside track.

She assumes the role of parent with her own children but does manage the discipline a bit differently. Although she applies the principle of being consistent with consequences, she lets down with her own children in a different way. Andrea also allows for quality to the give-and-take in their conversations that distinguishes her as the children's mother, not as their teacher.

Her professional skill and knowledge certainly gives Andrea an advantage, but Andrea realizes that her heart holds her own children in a special place reserved only for them. Her students are not competition to her own children. Each are important but are so in ways appropriate to their unique relationship with her.

Andrea also thinks about ways she will support her parents and spouse as they age. Since she has grown in assertiveness, knows how systems work, and has experienced supporting those at a disadvantage, she is certain that when any of her family or friends become physically or emotionally vulnerable, she will be effective. She knows she will be able to communicate their needs and give them the assistance and support that will best help them in whatever the circumstances.

While Andrea spends a good share of her energy communicating in the school environment, she also sustains friendships, some casual and temporary and others long term and for life. Just like at school, she knows how and where to set boundaries and meet her needs for confidential sharing and expression of her personal goals and dreams. She knows how to read both her close friends and acquaintances. Andrea knows what makes them laugh and what matters for many.

When with those in her extended casual social circle, Andrea chooses what matters might be sensitive and what would enhance her connection. Just like with her students, Andrea is reading the situation in a natural way, processing what she sees and hears, within and without. Then she speaks or holds back as seems appropriate for the person and situation.

Special education teachers have learned to relate successfully and effectively with challenging students. Beyond that, due to their inherent and well-developed communication skills, they relate well with students, parents, staff, family, and friends. In doing so, they receive the care and respect of those with whom they relate.

SUMMARY

While noticing and listening to the students, notice also your own responses and feelings relative to what you observe. Be present and respectful to students. Reinforce and discourage behaviors as you address and accept the ups and downs exhibited by students. While using good boundaries, show interest and care as you interpret student behaviors. Grounded in skilled behavioral understanding, you, as special educators, ably apply the skills integrated from working with students when communicating with staff, parents, family, friends, and in social relationships.

Chapter Five

Recognition of Positive Actions

Mr. Grey has been a special education teacher in a middle school cross-categorical classroom for fifteen years. He works hard to set high expectations for his students academically and behaviorally. He works with classroom teachers to make sure that his students are included in general education classrooms to the maximum extent appropriate. He encourages his students to succeed, and he "sets them up for success."

Throughout the years he has had some students that no one thought he would be able to reach. Yet with Mr. Grey's positive attitude and his belief that his students could succeed, he has made a difference for them.

He has learned to never take good behavior for granted—to always reinforce each step that the student takes on his or her road to success. Mr. Grey's philosophy is to teach the students the appropriate academic and behavioral skills so they don't fail. If a student makes an error in judgment or in academics, Mr. Grey provides constructive criticism and uses any negative event as an opportunity to teach the child a better way. Mr. Grey continually assesses his own role whenever a problem behavior occurs. He asks himself whether he accented positive behavior enough, whether he taught the student the appropriate skill, and what he can do differently in the future.

Mr. Grey learned early in his training about the importance of positive reinforcement. When he was in college, he was fortunate that his professors taught him that it was important to recognize the positive behavior that students exhibited. He also learned that it was important for him to provide multiple opportunities for the students to respond, and when they responded correctly, to reinforce them.

He has worked hard to monitor his use of praise within the classroom and has worked cooperatively with the paraprofessional assigned to him to assure that she also uses positive reinforcement. At least once a week, he tapes himself for thirty minutes to an hour and then takes the tape home and listens to it. He jots down the number of praise statements he gives and to whom. He also jots down the number of reprimands he gives to his students. If the reprimands exceed the praise statements, he knows he must work harder to praise his students more. If he notices that he rarely praises one of his students, he knows he must focus on being more positive to that student.

Mr. Grey has three children, ages three through twelve, of his own. He applies his principles of recognizing them for their positive behaviors when he gets home. When his twelve-year-old starts his homework, Mr. Grey praises him for his efforts and offers to assist him if needed. When his seven-year-old cleans the dishes off the table after dinner, he lets him know how much he appreciates that. When his three-year-old gets ready for bed on time, he is delighted and claps and tells her that he is so proud of her. Mr. Grey and his wife work as a team to recognize the positive actions of their children. Mr. Grey also recognizes the importance of supporting his wife for all the work she does.

In the classroom and in his home life, Mr. Grey has learned to never take good behavior for granted and to reinforce it. He looks for the positive in any event and praises what is right rather than focusing on what is wrong.

Colleagues at school and in the neighborhood love being around Mr. Grey because he has such a positive disposition.

Like Mr. Grey, good special educators know the importance of recognizing their students for positive actions. They look for what is right about what the student is doing rather than what the student may do wrong. They accept responsibility for setting the student up for success. They learn to see progress in small steps and to celebrate that progress. They attribute the student's progress to the actions of the student. This chapter focuses on how the special educator recognizes positive actions in the classroom and with other people in the individual's life.

THE IMPORTANCE OF REINFORCEMENT

Accenting the positive is the goal for all educators. It is very important, especially for special educators, because oftentimes students with disabilities have failed before they have received services and they need a boost in their confidence and self-esteem. Students in special education who have exhibited behavioral problems have been reprimanded many times and expect more of the same; it is critical that this expectation be changed. Students who have struggled academically have been faced with assignments that were too difficult for them and have become accustomed to failure. Because of that failure, they are not enthused about learning because it has been hard for them. Their expectation is one of failure, and the special educator must provide academic work that the student is able to do and provide reinforcement when the student is able to complete it.

At least 70 percent of the comments that the educator makes to the student each day should be positive statements (Johns and Carr, 2009); when the educator looks for the positive, the students feel better and the educator feels better because he or she is recognizing the achievements of the student. The special educator looks for the strengths of each student and capitalizes on those strengths. The special educator establishes a positive classroom climate where students want to be because they are successful and are frequently recognized for what they do right. They don't worry about making a mistake because the teacher is there to help them learn the right way. In life, people prefer to be around those who are positive and look for the good in a situation.

Recognition of Accomplishment and Effort

The special educator recognizes the student not only for accomplishments, which should be celebrated, but also for his or her efforts to accomplish a task. Because many of the students have had a history of failure, they have given up and don't even want to try to accomplish a task. Therefore, it is critical that the special educator provide recognition for effort. Even though the student may not be able to do the entire task, he should be recognized for the efforts that he or she has made to do the task.

As an example, the student may feel defeated before beginning a task and the special educator works to assure that the student is given work that he is able to handle. However, some students have developed emotional blocks toward certain academic tasks: "I hate math." "I don't like to read." These are common statements that may come from the mouths of students who come into special education. The special educator encourages the student to just start the task; when the student does start the task, his effort to do so should be praised by the special educator.

Special educators exhibit this disposition when they seek services for home or car repairs or with their families. When someone has successfully provided a service for them, they praise the effort and the accomplishment. We may have called someone to complete a repair, but when the person comes to do the repair he finds that it is too complex and someone else will need to be called to complete the repair. The special educator at least recognizes the effort of the individual to try to fix the problem.

Since the special educator has seen firsthand the many advantages of recognizing positive actions and uses that recognition on a regular basis, it becomes a habit and the educator applies that habit into his or her everyday life.

At home, the special educator's own children may have come in the door with homework in tow. The special educator scans the homework and recognizes that it may be difficult for her own child to do but knows the importance of recognizing the child for at least getting started on the assignment. The special educator may have elderly parents who need to be recognized when they remember to take their medication or go out and socialize with friends.

Behavior-specific Praise

The special educator has learned that praise is important, and even more effective is behavior-specific praise—telling the student or anyone else he or she is recognizing the specific behavior being recognized. As examples, behavior-specific praise would include such statements as "Thank you for raising your hand," "I really like the way you stood in line quietly," "I appreciate how you helped Elysha with that math problem."

Behavior-specific praise is more effective because it lets the student know exactly what you liked as opposed to general praise such as: "Good," "Great work," "Terrific." General praise is certainly better than no recognition, but behavior-specific praise will increase the likelihood that the desired behavior will continue and lets the student know exactly what the desired behavior was.

In working with the parents of the students with special needs, the special educator remembers that the parents have often been blamed for the challenges that their children have, they may have only received calls from the school when the student was in trouble, and they may be overwhelmed with the challenges that their child faces.

Oftentimes the parents don't receive a great deal of positive recognition for the work that they are doing to raise their child. The special educator realizes that, if he or she is going to establish a positive working relationship with the parent, he must be thankful for the efforts that the parent makes—to get the student to school each day, to help the student with homework, to respond to notes sent home. The special educator knows the importance of thanking the parent when he or she sees the parent, of writing positive notes home about how the student has done, of picking up the telephone and calling the parent to thank him or her for something nice the parent did. This provides a feeling of confidence and security on the part of the parent and establishes a true partnership in working together for the benefit of the child with special needs.

In everyday life, the special educator has become used to recognizing specific behavior and habitually lets people know when they have engaged in a desired behavior. The special educator not only praises his or her students but also uses behavior-specific praise when working with the paraprofessional who may be assigned to the class or a certain student. The special educator praises colleagues for doing kind actions, such as the school secretary when she does a task for him or her, or the custodian who picks up her garbage on a regular basis.

Attributions

Attribution is the way that an individual explains to himself the cause of his success or failure. Children who are poor achievers tend to attribute successes that they have to factors not within their control—luck or the teacher. Children who are successful achievers attribute success to their own efforts. Good special educators teach their students to become independent and to attribute their success to their efforts (Lerner and Johns, 2009).

How does the special educator get the student to change his or her attribution style? The special educator reinforces the student by specifically telling the student exactly what he or she did to succeed. As an example, the teacher says: "You got an A on that test because you really studied," or "You worked hard to complete that assignment and your hard work paid off." At times educators may forget to attribute the student's success to the child, but special educators are trained to teach their students what role their efforts had in what happened to them.

In life, individuals may want to attribute another individual's success to something that they did—"You were able to complete that knitting project because I helped you a lot with it," or "You had a good teacher." However, the special educator's response would be "You were able to complete that knitting project because you stuck with it and kept working on the project— your perseverance made a big difference."

Monitoring Your Own Use of Praise

The special educator has learned that there is a direct connection between his or her own behavior and the student's behavior. The more the teacher reprimands, the more the students act up. If the special educator has had a particularly rough day with the students, it is time to look at one's own behavior to see what went wrong. Did the teacher recognize the students for their appropriate behavior? Was the teacher particularly tense that day? Was the teacher preoccupied with other things and didn't attend to the needs of the students? Good special educators spend time at the end of the day reflecting on their own behavior. They may keep a journal of how the day went. Reflective practice is critical in the area of special education.

There are a number of ways that the special educator can monitor his/her use of praise. The special educator may opt to audiotape himself or herself.

Remember that Mr. Grey chose to audiotape himself by picking a thirty-minute block of time that he noticed was a difficult time of day for him and the students. He then took the tape home and listened to it, marking down the number of general praise statements he made, the number of behavior-specific praise statements he used, and the number of reprimands he gave. He knew that at least 70 percent of his statements to his students should be positive statements. If he had not met that goal during the tape, then he set a goal for himself to work to achieve it the next time he taped. If one also notices that certain students are being praised a great deal and others are not receiving much praise at all, the teacher should work to make sure that the student not receiving much praise receives more.

Special educators may also want to videotape themselves within the classroom and then critique the video after class to analyze their own behavior.

Some special educators also have used the penny-in-my-pocket technique, in which they put a certain number of pennies in one pocket at the beginning of the day. Each time they make a praise statement to a student, they move one of the pennies from the one pocket to the other one. The goal is to move all the pennies from one pocket to another.

Because special educators know the importance of providing frequent positive reinforcement to their students, they may have established a ticket reinforcement system within their classroom that also allows them to monitor their use of reinforcement. The special educator has a supply of raffle tickets. Each time he or she sees that a student is behaving appropriately, he gives the student a ticket while also praising the student for the specific behavior. At the end of the day, there is a drawing of tickets for a prize or prizes. The special educator can designate a specific number that he or she plans to distribute that day, and the goal is to assure that all of the tickets are distributed to students.

In life's situations, the special educator reflects on events that happen to assure that he or she is recognizing people for their positive actions. Did I remember to thank the friendly clerk at the grocery store? Did I remember to thank the person who bagged my groceries? If a relationship that I have with another individual is strained, have I engaged in positive interactions with that individual?

SETTING STUDENTS UP FOR SUCCESS
THROUGH ERRORLESS LEARNING

The goal of the special educator is to assure the student's success and keep any mistakes or errors to a minimum. Once a student has learned something wrong it is harder to unlearn and relearn correctly, so the special educator is always striving to assure a reduction in student errors. The special educator wants to set the student up for success by assuring that the student gets the correct response the first time the response is requested.

Such errorless learning applies to both behavior and academic skills. It is very easy for a child to learn inappropriate behavior, particularly when the student has been in settings where the adults have not been consistent with the student. In the real world, sometimes when students act up they may be corrected but at other times, the adult lets the behavior slide.

Different educators tolerate different behaviors. One educator may allow the students to talk in the school hallways. Another educator may not tolerate that behavior. If the student has been in class with the teacher who allows the student to talk in the hallway, then a behavior pattern has been established. When the student is in the classroom of the teacher who does not allow talking in the hallway, the student will have a more difficult time learning not to talk because he learned previously he could talk in the hallway.

Think about those individuals who never learned to type and use the hunt-and-peck method when they need to type something. When those individuals then try to learn correct keyboarding it is even more difficult for them because they learned it the wrong way and now have to unlearn and correctly learn keyboarding.

Reinforcing Successive Approximations: Looking for Progress in Small Steps

Special educators have learned that their students come to them having already failed in academic and behavioral areas. They know that their students have learned incorrect academic responses and inappropriate social behaviors. They know that it will take time for their students to unlearn and learn correctly. They focus on the most problematic behaviors and the academic skills where the student struggles the most. Critically, they know that miracles don't happen overnight. The children didn't get the way they are quickly, and the academics and behavior won't be changed quickly—it will take time and a great deal of effort.

As a result of this realization, they learn to see progress in small steps and to celebrate with the student the little things that put the student on the road to success. They therefore reinforce the student for successive approximations to the goals they want to meet with the student. The special educator establishes goals for the student and then sets short-term objectives or benchmarks to achieve those goals. They break the task into small steps and reinforce the student for achieving each small step.

They task analyze each skill—whether it be a behavioral skill or an academic skill—that they want the child to achieve and then reinforce the successive approximations to get there.

Oftentimes, we may forget the complexity of a task we expect a student to complete; task analysis forces us to look at that complexity and break it down into small, achievable steps. One of the authors remembers vividly in her early teaching days working with a student who was nonverbal and trying to get him to say some basic words. The first step was to get him to make a consonant sound. She still remembers to this day the thrill and pleasure that she and the student had when he first made the "M" sound. To others, this would not seem important, but to her and this student it was a great day—the child had been reinforced for successive approximations to the goal.

Recently, one of the authors had taken a group of college students to observe in a classroom for students with severe and profound cognitive disabilities. The teacher explained that the students were working on responding to what kind of weather it was. She first worked with the students on gazing out the window to look at what was happening outside. When the students would look out the window, she would praise them—again reinforcing successive approximations.

Special educators succeed because they can analyze the task and see progress in small steps. Small achievements that other educators would take for granted are never taken for granted by the special educator—they are celebrated. Because of the importance of this skill, we devote an entire chapter about this topic of being able to see progress in small steps.

Special educators carry this disposition over into their everyday life. They may have their own children, and they expect their children to clean their rooms. Most children are resistant to this activity—they would rather be doing other, more exciting, tasks. However, the parent has learned that if the child does one activity that is integral to cleaning the room, he or she should praise the child. Praising will then motivate the child to do more work in the room.

Teaching the Correct Response or Behavior

Before expecting a student to provide a correct academic response, the special educator knows that he or she must teach the skill, model the correct response, provide plenty of opportunities for practice, and provide reinforcement for giving the correct answer. This is also true when establishing behavioral expectations—the special educator always teaches the appropriate response in a given situation, models the appropriate behavior, provides plenty of opportunities for practice, and reinforces the student when the student exhibits the appropriate behavior.

When a student has difficulty mastering a skill, the teacher knows that she must provide more instruction and provide more opportunities for practice. When the special educator has taught a given lesson and a student asks a question about the lesson, the special educator recognizes that more direct instruction of the skill is needed. Again, the teacher is always assessing whether she has taught the student the skill.

If a student engages in an inappropriate behavior, the special educator asks himself or herself whether the student actually knew the correct behavior. If the student did not have the skill to engage in the appropriate behavior, then the teacher must provide direct instruction to teach the skill. As an example, if a young student wants a toy from another child and goes up and just grabs the toy, the teacher uses this as an opportunity to teach a skill—if another child has a toy you want, how do you go to the student and ask politely whether you can play with the toy?

It is critical that we remember to teach the appropriate behavior or academic skill before the student has the opportunity to make an error. A critical way to do that is to teach the correct response before the student ever has the chance to give an inappropriate response.

The special educator can have special insight into the behavior of fellow adults—recognizing that somewhere along the line, the individuals may not have been taught the appropriate behavior and that is the reason they behave the way they do. As an example, we have all known adults who have never learned the social skill of how to accept a compliment. When you give them a compliment, they say something negative about what you said. You may say: "I really like that jacket you are wearing." The colleague replies: "Oh, it's something ugly I had in the closet." It is important that you continue to provide compliments to the individual but at the same time model how you accept a compliment and recognize them when they do accept your compliment appropriately.

Precorrection

The use of precorrection is a critical component of errorless learning for behavior as well as in academics. Educators use precorrection for academic skills frequently—when they see that it is likely that a student is coming to a word in reading that the student does not know, the teacher will correctly state the word so that the student is given the right answer and can be successful. When the teacher gives a math problem that he or she sees might be difficult for the student, he or she will assist the student in getting the correct answer. The educator can then recognize the student for getting the right answer.

The special educator knows the importance of precorrection for behavior as well. As Kauffman and Landrum (2009) state: "Strong reinforcement for

appropriate behavior is important, but precorrection begins with examina-
tion of the context in which misbehavior is likely and how conditions might
be altered and instructional (as opposed to correctional) procedures used to
prevent the misbehavior from occurring—how triggers and agitation can be
avoided" (p. 302). When the educator looks at problem contexts and behavior
that might be likely to occur because of those contexts, the teacher can change
the context and can also rehearse with the student what the student should do
in the given situation.

As an example, when Marcus is going out to recess and Jimmy, from
another class, is out there, Marcus goes up to Jimmy and calls him names
because Jimmy calls him names first. If the teacher wants to precorrect the
behavior, the teacher can send the rest of the class out to recess with another
staff member and stay behind with Marcus. She can talk with Marcus about
what he can do when Jimmy calls him names. She can then practice with
Marcus appropriate responses to Jimmy. She lets Marcus know that she believes he can move away from Jimmy and not call him names. She then walks
out to recess with Marcus and reminds him calmly that she knows he can do
the right thing. When Marcus walks away from Jimmy when Jimmy calls him
a name, she calls Marcus over and reinforces him for his positive action.

In life, we use precorrection when we are working with our own children
by preparing them for difficult situations. We might also use precorrection
with an elderly relative when we know that the relative is going into what
could be a difficult situation for him or her to handle.

Prompting and Fading

When we want our students to have the opportunity to be recognized for
positive actions, we need to prompt them to engage in the desired behavior
or to provide the correct response. In sequential prompting, the special educator uses multiple levels of prompts in order from maximum cues to minimal
cues. There is a strong evidence base for such techniques, particularly at the
secondary level (Ryan, Pierce, and Mooney, 2008).

The teacher provides prompts to assure that the student will be successful.
As an example, when the teacher wants to assure that the student will be able to
read a word correctly, the teacher will hold up the picture of the word before the
student has to read it. When the teacher is teaching the student what the classroom rules mean, the teacher will pair the rules with pictures of the rules—these
are prompts that assist the student in providing a correct response.

One form of prompting is fading. In this process, the teacher provides maximum cues for the student and then fades those cues away until the student is
able to do the task on his or her own (Johns, 2004). One method of fading is

used when teaching the student cursive writing. The teacher provides a model of the letter to be written and the child is expected to trace over the letter. The teacher then recognizes the student for tracing over the letter. The teacher can then prepare a model with dotted lines, and the student traces over the dotted lines. The last step is when the student is able to write the letter on his own (Lerner and Johns, 2009).

Special educators provide multiple opportunities to respond for students. They present information in such a way that it increases students' correct responding. As an example, when the student is learning a new letter such as "B," the teacher holds up the letter "B." The teacher says: "This is a 'B.' What letter is this?" The student then responds correctly after the teacher has prompted the student with the correct letter.

When educators increase the rates of the opportunity to respond, they see increases in on-task student behavior, more correct responses, and fewer disruptive behaviors (Conroy, Sutherland, Snyder, and Marsh, 2008).

Special educators use prompting and fading techniques throughout their everyday life in an effort to assure the success of individuals with whom they work or live. Special educators prompt family members to give a correct response.

In the case of assuring the success of an aging parent who has difficulty remembering something that needs to be done, the special educator may write notes for his or her parent to help the parent remember. For the aging parent who is struggling with memory problems, this is most appreciated and prevents unneeded frustration for the parent.

Modeling

A critical component in teaching is modeling. The special educator is the role model for the student and knows that it is critical that we adopt the adage "Do as I say and as I do." In order for the special educator to teach the child the importance of the recognition of positive actions, the special educator must provide that recognition to the students on a frequent basis. Children then become accustomed to a positive classroom environment—a pleasant environment where the children want to be.

Our actions speak loud and clear to the student that we are looking for appropriate behavior and looking for the good, rather than the bad. The teacher should also praise the students when they are caught praising their peers.

Many special educators have established a system in which the students are given note cards and at the end of the day or a given period of time, the students should write down a compliment that they observed that day for each of their classmates.

SUMMARY

Setting up students for success is the mantra for the special educator. Special educators set high expectations for their students and work with them to assure their success. By establishing such a positive climate and excitement for learning, the special educator then provides recognition for all the positive actions that the students achieve each and every day.

Children want to come to school when they know they are going to succeed and be recognized for that success. Children feel a sense of accomplishment, and they know that the special educator is there to help them achieve their goals.

With such challenges facing our society and facing our students, children need to have a haven where they are accepted and recognized. Children learn firsthand the importance of having a positive attitude because it has been modeled by the special educator in and outside the classroom. A positive attitude is a mainstay for a happy, healthy, and productive life.

REFERENCES

Conroy, M., Sutherland, K., Snyder, A., and Marsh, S. (2008). Classwide interventions: Effective instruction makes a difference. *Teaching exceptional children, 40(6)*, 24–30.

Johns, B., and Carr, V. (2009). *Techniques for managing verbally and physically aggressive students*. 3rd ed. Denver: Love Publishing Company.

Johns, B. (2004). Practical behavioral strategies for students with autism. *The Journal of Safe Management of Disruptive and Assaultive Behavior, 12(2)*, 6–11.

Kauffman, J., and Landrum, T. (2009). *Characteristics of emotional and behavioral disorders of children and youth*. 9th ed. Upper Saddle River, New Jersey: Pearson Education.

Lerner, J., and Johns, B. (2009). *Learning disabilities and related mild disabilities: Characteristics, teaching strategies, and new directions*. Boston: Houghton Mifflin Harcourt Publishing Company.

Ryan, J., Pierce, C., and Mooney, P. (2008). Evidence-based teaching strategies for students with EBD. *Beyond Behavior, 17(3)*, 22–29.

Chapter Six

Addressing Discipline Challenges

Mrs. Bischof has worked with high school students with behavioral disorders for ten years—people are always asking her why she wants to work with her students. Many don't understand how a small lady who weighs only a hundred pounds and is five feet tall can possibly work with these students. Colleagues within the school and in the community are always asking her how she can discipline students who are so much bigger than she is. Mrs. Bischof always replies that she treats her students with respect, and they respect her back.

She tells them that she views discipline as teaching. She teaches her students the expectations; she is firm, fair, and consistent. She also looks for warning signs that her students are becoming frustrated and teaches them the socially acceptable behaviors. Most importantly, she teaches her students to identify the triggers that upset them and how to appropriately handle those triggers. She has never been hit by a student and has very few discipline challenges because of the proactive approach she has used throughout the years.

Previous teachers were afraid of these students; Mrs. Bischof is not. She views her students as important human beings who face challenges and sees herself as there to help them overcome those challenges. Mrs. Bischof does not see discipline as punishment but views it as an opportunity to teach the students a better way to deal with their problems. She believes that consequences should be logical and should teach students.

Mrs. Bischof has four children of her own and has adopted her well-ingrained discipline philosophy with them. She teaches them her expectations, the rules of the house are posted on the refrigerator, she talks to her children privately when they have exhibited behavioral concerns, and she is always reflecting on how she has handled a situation to determine whether she could have done something differently.

Mrs. Bischof and her husband are also building a new home, and she has learned quickly that her discipline techniques are applicable to those involved in the building project. As an example, the carpet layer made an error in the carpet—leaving a lump in the middle of the new living room. Mrs. Bischof and her husband were upset but remained calm and told the carpet layer clearly that the carpet was not acceptable. It would need to be removed and redone or there would not be any payment for the work. They gave the carpet layer the opportunity to do the work correctly; otherwise, there would be no payment. Because they were reasonable and calm, the carpet layer took the carpeting up and put it down correctly.

Students who exhibit behavioral problems challenge school personnel. These students require discipline that involves prevention and teaching appropriate skills so that students learn through the process. Special educators have learned the importance of preventing behavioral problems before they occur and have also learned that when a student does need to be disciplined, it should be designed to teach the student a more appropriate way to deal with the behavior.

AN OUNCE OF PREVENTION

"Waiting for students to fail before you intervene is one of the most passive stances you can take as a teacher" (Jackson, 2009, p. 104).

In the previous chapter, we discussed the importance of setting students up for success. We don't want students to fail by having discipline issues. Instead, we want them to succeed by establishing the means for them to do so. We must work to prevent discipline problems rather than causing them.

Good special educators have learned to look for warning signs that a student is becoming frustrated, and they then provide supportive assistance to prevent a problem. They know important strategies like active listening and empathy (discussed in an earlier chapter), they use proximity control and high degrees of supervision to know firsthand what is actually occurring, they teach students deep-breathing techniques to calm themselves down, they use a calm voice when they are speaking to the student, and they are nonconfrontational in their approach. These techniques are preventive.

Such techniques serve the special educator well in real-life situations outside the classroom. The special educator may have to deal with an angry parent, and a calm approach will go much further in working with the parent, rather than becoming angry and confrontational. The special educator may go to a show or be in a grocery store and meet someone who is angry because they wanted the seat the special educator was occupying or they got the last of an item in the store and the person is angry. The special educator deals with the situation in a calm manner in order to prevent a potentially volatile situation.

Firm, Fair, and Consistent

It is critical that special educators have the philosophy that they must be firm with their students. Teachers set limits for students so students learn the boundaries in given situations. They are firm without being mean. They don't make idle threats to students—"If you don't get this done, you are going to stay at school until you get it done." However, the teacher doesn't have the time to stay after school and can't carry through with what he said. When teachers make idle threats to students, the student loses trust in the adult. They know that the teacher doesn't do what the teacher says he or she will do.

Special educators carefully think about what they are going to say before they say it to the student. One of the authors knew a special educator who told her about a situation that occurred with one of his students. He became angry with the student and made an idle threat to the student that he could not implement. It took over a year to regain the trust of the student. The student had learned that he couldn't trust what the teacher said because of that one incident. The teacher must be firm while being kind and respectful—clarity in what the teacher wants from the student is a must.

Students have a real sense of fairness. If they perceive that certain students are given special privileges because of who they are, they will see that the teacher is not being fair. If two students engage in an inappropriate behavior and one student's parent is a friend of the teacher or the student's parent is on the school board, the educator may be tempted to give the one student a special break. The other student is given a harsher consequence. This is not fair to either student—the one who got the special privilege (because it is teaching him that he can "get away" with certain behaviors because of who he is) and the other student who got a harsher consequence than he should have.

Special educators work to achieve consistency in their approach. This is one of the most difficult challenges that all educators face because we are human beings. Some days we might tolerate certain behaviors; other days we are not in the mood to deal with those behaviors and provide harsher consequences. It is important that educators realize that they must work continually to assure that they are consistent with their students. Students with special needs must have an environment that is structured and consistent and where they know exactly what is expected. They don't do well in environments where they are guessing what will be expected of them. Most of us don't do well in settings where we don't know what is expected of us.

Discipline with Respect

Working with students in special education requires the establishment of a trusting relationship with the students. In order to do that, the educator must treat the student with respect in order to earn the respect of the student. The special educator is very conscious of the importance of treating students with dignity. When a student is showing signs of frustration, the special educator addresses the situation privately; he or she does not confront an issue publicly in front of the students' peers. Just as we adults want to be treated with respect, so does the student. No adult wants to be confronted in front of other adults—this is embarrassing, and we lose respect for those people who choose to reprimand us publicly. Such behavior is a form of bullying. When a student has a problem, it is critical that the adult talk with the student privately. Students need to save face—they aren't being afforded that opportunity when we publicly embarrass them.

Public redirection of children may reinforce the viewpoint that they are problem students, and this can be a self-fulfilling prophecy. It may also intensify the challenging behaviors. Students have to save face, and when public reprimands are given, the teacher is setting the student up to misbehave. Redirection should be presented in a kind and nonchallenging manner that is more likely to result in a positive response (Farmer, Goforth, Hives, Aaron, Jackson, and Sgammato, 2006).

Special educators are very conscious of issues surrounding confidentiality and respect the need to keep a situation about one student private from other students. Special educators have learned to respect the right to privacy of their colleagues. When they are upset by an action that was taken by a colleague, they talk to that individual one-to-one rather than talking to them in front of other people.

Assessing the Discipline Problem: Functional Assessment

When students are exhibiting academic problems, good special education teachers assess the problem. They look closely at what level the child is achieving and what particular weaknesses are preventing the student from learning. Just as in academics, good teachers also assess behavior. They look closely at where the student is—what specific problems are being presented and what weaknesses are preventing the student from engaging in the appropriate behavior. Functional assessment looks thoroughly at the student's behavior—not just jumping to conclusions about the behavior but really taking an in-depth look at what is happening.

All behavior serves a function. Students engage in certain behaviors to fulfill an unmet need. There are three major functions of behavior—access, escape/avoidance, or sensory issues. Some students engage in a specific behavior in order to seek access to attention or power and control. Some students want attention, and they will engage in behaviors to seek either positive or negative attention. When students are engaging in behaviors because they are seeking attention, it will be critical for the teacher to recognize that so the teacher can provide attention in a positive way.

Some students engage in behaviors in order to escape or avoid a specific task or a specific setting. For instance, the student may believe that the math work is too hard and therefore he gets sick and asks to go to the nurse's office rather than participate in math. The student might also tear up his math paper when it is time to do math. If the teacher were to tell the student to go to the office, the teacher would be allowing the student to escape the math task. When students are engaging in specific behaviors during a given academic period, it is critical that the teacher look at the work that is being expected of the student to determine whether the work is too difficult, there is too much work at one time, or the student may be embarrassed that he or she will fail in front of peers.

The last function of behavior deals with sensory issues. We know that some students are bothered by specific sensory issues—as an example, if the student is bothered by loud noises, he may want to avoid going to the cafeteria. Some students are bothered by flickering fluorescent lights, and the teacher may need to either put a cover over the lights or provide a lamp for the student to diffuse the light. Some students may be bothered by certain textures of clothes and are frustrated and act out.

Good special educators are detectives. When a behavior occurs, they try to figure out why the student is doing what he or she does. The behavior serves an unmet need, and the special educator who can pinpoint the student's needs can resolve many discipline problems.

Functional assessment carefully considers the cultural background of the student. Is the student engaging in specific behaviors because of cultural differences? A teacher can easily cause an altercation with a student when demanding that a student look her in the eye when she is talking to him or her; however, perhaps the student's culture sees that as a sign of disrespect, not respect.

It is important for the special educator to view the function of behavior by examining sociocultural factors surrounding the student (Preciado, Horner, and Baker, 2009). The teacher needs to understand that the student may have a different set of expectations within his home culture than he does within the school culture. Inappropriate behavior cannot be accepted, but it is important to understand the reasons a student may behave as he does. The special educator knows that he or she has to teach the expectations within the school setting because those expectations are different than what they may be at home.

In another example, a student may have been abused as a young child and becomes very upset when the teacher puts a hand on him or her even though it is done in a positive way. A child who was locked in a dark closet as a young child may become very fearful when he is in a dark area.

Medical issues are also a critical consideration in functional assessment. The special educator knows that the student with ADHD needs to be afforded the opportunity to move around frequently; to expect the student to sit in a desk for long periods of time will result in discipline problems. The student may be causing discipline problems because he has a fluctuating hearing loss and is frustrated because he can't understand what the teacher or other students are saying. The student with diabetes may be acting out because his blood sugar is not regulated.

Functional assessment is a critical component in understanding specific problem behaviors that the student is exhibiting. Behavior is communication, and when a student is exhibiting recurring discipline problems the special educator works to analyze the multiple dimensions of behavior.

Special educators find themselves using functional assessment in everyday situations. They may encounter a boss who yells or points his finger in their face. That boss may want access to power and control. They find that their elderly parent is avoiding large-group situations. The function of the parent's behavior might be escape/avoidance because the parent has failing hearing. A friend becomes easily upset, and the special educator learns that the individual's diabetes is out of control.

DISCIPLINE IS NOT PUNITIVE; IT IS ALL ABOUT TEACHING

Many individuals and some school personnel feel the need to punish students when they have gotten into trouble. They don't understand the important mind-set that discipline should not be about punishment. For long-lasting changes in behavior, discipline is about teaching. Punishment eliminates problem behavior quickly but breeds resentment on the part of the student and does not result in meaningful, positive change for the student. Special educators understand that it is their job to teach, not punish.

Establishing and Enforcing Clear Expectations

When students exhibit discipline problems, the special educator reflects on whether the student specifically knew the expectations of the setting. As an example, Joe has moved to a new school and is caught running in the hall. Certainly this behavior is not appropriate for the student, but since the student is new to the school, educators must ask themselves whether the student knew the expectation. Perhaps he was in the habit of running in the hall in his previous school, and he was allowed to do so. If so, Joe has to be taught that such behavior is not acceptable in his new school.

Expectations must be taught, posted, and reviewed frequently. Students must also be reinforced when they follow the rules. When students know exactly what is expected of them, they are less likely to exhibit discipline problems. If the rule is "Respect Others," then students have to be taught what that looks like—it means keeping one's hands to himself, it means talking appropriately to other students and adults. When rules are posted, it is preferable that a picture or a picture cue be paired with the written rule. That way, the student can see what the rule looks like. Let's look again at the example of Joe. If the hallway rules are posted and the rule is "Walk in the Hall," then there can be a picture beside the words that shows a student walking in the hall. This could be a photograph or a drawn picture.

Special educators know the importance of clear rules stated positively and posted in the room. They also know that the rules must be reviewed periodically, and when students are following the rules, they need to be reinforced for following the rules.

"Rather than viewing rules as elements of control, rules might best be conceptualized as contributing to a classroom environment conducive to learning" (Kostewicz, Ruhl, and Kubina, 2008, p. 14). Special educators have learned that posting the rules can diffuse difficult situations. The special educator might see the student having a problem and the special educator can say: "What do you need to do to follow rule #3?"

In everyday life, we all have to abide by rules and want to know what the rules are in a given situation. Families may have the household rules posted. When people go to the library, they see the signs posted that talking is to be done quietly.

Teaching Appropriate Behaviors

Because discipline should be about teaching, special educators know that just as we teach academics, we also teach appropriate behavior. Before we can teach academics, we have learned that we need to assess the skills of the students. Before we can teach behavior, we must also assess the skill level of the student.

In behavior, students may have a skill deficit—meaning that they have not learned the skill at all. Students could also have a performance deficit—they have learned the skill but they don't practice the skill. Another option is that the student has a fluency deficit—meaning he or she has learned the skill, practice it, but it is not natural or easy for the child. The special educator knows that when she observes a student engaging in a problematic behavior, she must figure out whether the child has a skill deficit, a performance deficit, or a fluency deficit. If the special educator is not sure, generally she will assume it is a skill deficit and teach the child directly the appropriate behavior.

In life, we encounter individuals who don't know how to behave in a certain situation. They have never learned the skill. Special educators find themselves seeing these people in a variety of environments and letting them know what is expected of them. They may model the appropriate behavior, or they may see that someone is becoming upset about a situation. They work to diffuse the situation. Let's take this example. A teacher goes to a baby shower for a fellow teacher. One of the individuals who was invited is very volatile and gets upset easily and can't always deal with her anger. The teacher who is in attendance notices that the volatile individual is getting upset because she is not receiving a lot of attention. The special educator approaches the individual and calmly asks her if she will help her carry some of the dishes into the kitchen. The individual agrees and learns that removing herself from an upsetting situation for just a few minutes helps diffuse the tension she is feeling.

Using a Discipline Problem as the Teachable Moment

Good special educators never miss an opportunity to teach the student a better way to deal with their problems. This is done through the teachable moment, problem solving (Johns and Carr, 2009). At times, educators will provide a consequence to a student when the student misbehaves and then drop the issue. The discipline incident should be used as an opportunity to teach the student. When the student is calm and the consequence for the inappropriate behavior has been given, it is time to process the event with the student. The special educator talks with the student, asking the following three questions: Tell me what happened? What did you do? What could you do the next time it happens?

Taking the time to ask these questions of the student allows the student to reflect on what happened and what the student's role was in the problem. The third question assists the student in thinking about more appropriate ways he or she can handle a similar situation if it were to recur. The special educator leads the student in reflection.

When a discipline issue is over, it should be over. Special educators do not hold grudges—they recognize the student made a mistake, they provide a consequence, they engage the student in the teachable moment, and then the incident is over. A teacher might be tempted to say to a student the next morning when he comes in to school: "Well, I hope you don't have the problems you had yesterday." Such a statement is inappropriate. Teachers are role models and show children that when an incident is over, it does not need to be brought up again with the student. It is forgotten, and it is time to move ahead.

We all know adults who hold grudges and never forget an action that another person took that was not favorable to them. It is not healthy to hold those grudges, and the special educator has learned firsthand that after an incident has been resolved, it should be forgotten.

Logical Consequences That Teach

Effective special educators know that it is important that students receive consequences for inappropriate behavior. Such consequences should be logical and designed to teach the student. Consequences that are related to what the student did are most effective. As an example, if a student has destroyed a piece of property or has made a mess in the lunchroom, the logical consequence would be for the student to repair the property or to clean up what he or she did. Such a consequence teaches the student a life-long skill that if you destroy something, you should repair it. It also teaches students more respect for property and a pride in the student's surroundings. As another example, if a student has called another student a name, a logical consequence would be an apology to that student and that the student write a list of compliments about the student who he called a name. This teaches the student the importance of focusing on the positive assets of the student rather than the negative attributes of the individual.

A common problem in today's schools with the increasing use of technology and student access to computers is that students may use the computer inappropriately. The logical consequence is to remove the computer privileges of the student for a set amount of time. The student learns that a computer should be used for productive rather than nonproductive activities (Johns and Carr, 2007).

TEACHING CHILDREN SELF-DISCIPLINE THROUGH SELF-MANAGEMENT

The ultimate goal for special educators is to teach children to monitor and manage their own behavior through a series of self-management strategies.

We want students to control their own behavior rather than relying on an adult to control that behavior. Special educators work to teach their students how to identify the behaviors that they need to improve. They then have students monitor those behaviors throughout the school day to see if they are increasing their appropriate behaviors.

Special educators teach students self-management in a number of ways. These are just a few:

1. Goal setting is an effective part of self-management. It is important that students set short-term and long-term goals for themselves and write down those goals. When special educators are working with students, they want to encourage the student to write down a goal they want to achieve for the morning. The goal is posted at the student's desk. They then set aside time for the student to evaluate whether they reached the goal. What a feeling of accomplishment when the goal is achieved! As students get used to setting goals, special educators can then have them write a daily goal or goals and then write weekly goals.

2. Checklists for students to assist them in controlling their own behavior are another form of self-management. These checklists can then be reviewed after the morning or at the end of the day to see whether the student was able to succeed. As an example, if a student has had difficulty controlling his anger when given an academic assignment, a checklist might be developed that would look like this:

   a. Did I review the assignment first before asking for help?
   b. Did I ask for help in the classroom when I didn't understand an assignment?
   c. Did I remember to raise my hand to ask for help?

3. Students should self-manage by using self-evaluation. Students actually evaluate their own academic and behavioral work to determine whether they have done what they set out to do.

4. Graphing their own progress is another tool of self-management. Students can graph their own progress and see whether they are controlling their own behaviors. It is rewarding for the student to see his or her own progress.

Special educators apply self-management skills in their own lives. If they want to lose weight, they set a goal for weight loss. If their friends want to lose weight, they encourage those individuals to set goals. They chart progress and celebrate that progress.

SUMMARY

The best approach to discipline is about teaching the child appropriate behavior and giving children the skills to identify the triggers that lead to discipline challenges and to proactively solve their own problems. Discipline should not be about punishment but should be designed to assist the student in learning the appropriate behavior. Any disciplinary event should be viewed as an opportunity to teach the child a better way to handle a problem.

REFERENCES

Farmer, T., Goforth, J., Hives, J., Aaron, A., Jackson, F., and Sgammato, A. (2006). Competence enhancement behavior management. *Preventing school failure, 50(3),* 39–44.

Jackson, R. (2009). *Never work harder than your students and other principles of great teaching.* Alexandria, Virginia: ASCD.

Johns, B., and Carr, V. (2009). *Techniques for managing verbally and physically aggressive students.* 3rd ed. Denver: Love Publishing.

Johns, B., and Carr, V. (2007). *Reduction of school violence: Alternatives to suspension.* 3rd ed. Horsham, Pennsylvania: LRP Publications.

Kostewicz, D., Ruhl, K., and Kubina, R. (2008). Creating classroom rules for students with emotional and behavioral disorders: A decision-making guide. *Beyond Behavior, 17(3),* 14–21.

Chapter Seven

The Ability to Create Individualized Educational Plans for Students

Cathy worked as a special educator through many eras of IEP designs. Now as an experienced teacher, she looks back to the first ones she did. Those she wrote for her students were done with ballpoint pen in carbon copies. She pulled them apart, keeping the two layers for the school and giving one to the parents. She remembers feeling that this was something she had to do but was not too closely tied to the process. She wrote very generally and kept her statements simple.

She recalls with mixed feelings the time Mrs. Hammond confronted her about her IEP writing style, saying Cathy's IEPs were not specific enough for her child, Bobby. This stunned Cathy at the time because she did not think including detail was essential. After all, when teaching, she followed her instincts and used appropriate methodology for her students. However, Mrs. Hammond was a strong advocate for her child and well-connected in the special education parent community. She belonged to an advocacy group and even attended IEP meetings as an official advocate to support parents seeking to gain better and more appropriate service for their children.

Though this parent put Cathy on the spot, Cathy asked that her coordinator get involved and meet with her and Mrs. Hammond. The result was a fast learning curve for Cathy and for the entire department. This spurred the coordinator to do training for everyone on writing more exact and effective IEPs.

As time went on Cathy saw the value of writing precision IEPs geared for each student. Even though she grouped students together, she specialized her objectives and benchmarks within small-group instruction. She learned to watch students more carefully during the testing process and noted her observations on the IEP. Once a child qualified for special education she gathered data and made informal observations, gearing up for conferences and for writing the next IEP.

When IEP goal and objective banks became a part of her district's practice, Cathy felt somewhat tempted to return to a form of "cookie-cutter" IEPs again. After all, the parents did not know what she included in another child's IEP. Yet, she heard her coordinator reinforce the idea that these were to be done with exactness and were to be connected with the needs of each child. It seemed to her that it was worth a try to put effort and energy into each IEP she crafted.

INDIVIDUALIZATION

In order for teachers like Cathy to individualize IEPs, they must be astute and work to know and accurately represent the needs of each student. Following are three areas to consider when crafting IEPs to specifically fit each child.

1. Test and teach with a heightened awareness. During the testing process a teacher may become tempted to move through the test quickly just to get done. After all, special educators experience a great demand on their time. However, when a teacher watches the child, looking for more than the correct answer on an academic test, they will be able to put together a fuller picture of the child's academic profile.

By having a notebook handy to jot down observations or by writing in the test booklet, an astute teacher will be able to keep account of a variety of details. The child sends many messages. The teacher is only to watch carefully for these signals and log them accurately throughout the testing period.

When you are testing, do you look for letter reversals, spoken and written language patterns, age-appropriate social speech, immature pencil grip, reading rate, the application of phonic skills, and the ability to read memorized nonphonetic words? Does the child appear comfortable with specific academic tasks? Does the student know math facts or count on her fingers? Does the student go through each step in a complex math problem? If not, at what point does the process break down?

What bogs down a student when taking a timed test? What causes him to appear pressured when tested? Is it hard for her to sit for a determined amount of time? Does visual acuity seem to be a problem? Does the student seem to go blank due to lack of information or apparent anxious feelings?

How might the student indicate any gaps in functional skills? Does she know how to tell time? Is he capable of following a personal schedule? When speaking about making a purchase, does she understand the value of common items? Does the youth have a job outside of school hours? What does the student do to assist in the classroom?

During breaks between subtests, does the child share anything personal that may have social or emotional significance? Does written-test content share anything that signals affective red flags, such as significant fears of fixation on extreme violence? Does the child appear well-cared-for at home? Is the child hungry? Has she had breakfast? Who are his friends? What does the young person reveal about having an adult support system?

Some of the information gathered during testing will apply directly to the IEP writing. Other information would be better shared with the classroom teacher, parents, or school personnel as appropriate.

2. Listen to other teachers and parents. Before and during the prereferral process, teachers will likely be advocating for the student by showing you work samples, sharing anecdotal information, and providing actual classroom tests that indicate the nature of the academic struggles at hand. You may be able to take one look at a spelling test and see the level of phonetic skills that a student has acquired or to pick up on a lack of visual memory just by how the child spells words that should be easily memorized if language abilities were intact.

A teacher's comments on how a child reads orally or recalls a story or facts in a science lesson offer helpful detail on ability to recall and apply information. A math paper or writing sample will tell you similar things about how a student processes information and what he can retain in terms of memorization.

Although the lounge is not the proper place for teachers to disclose the challenges and struggles of students for all to hear, it does happen that they do unload to one another in that environment. When a special educator overhears these discussions about students outside of his current caseload, it would be wise to file this anecdotal information away for future reference. Likely the teachers are talking about some students who will potentially be referred for special services at some point. This also gives perspective as to how students receiving service and those without such support compare academically, socially, behaviorally, and functionally.

Parents reveal concerns to classroom teachers on a regular basis. A teacher gathering data for prereferral will often provide information shared by a parent that could never be gained at school. This could come from parental experience with a child's frustrations as she periodically blows off steam at home and yet acts "normal" at school. This clue signals to adults that the child needs support in some area of curriculum or in the affective domain.

Parents will also provide official information from medical reports and test results from outside agencies. Much factual information from these reports can be directly added to the sections on the IEP that describe the student's current situation and those that provide descriptions of present levels of academic achievement and functional performance.

3. Design the IEP according to what you have learned about the child's academic, social, emotional, and functional needs. At this point a special educator has much information to sort through to describe student need as well as plan the IEP with the team.

Before going to the team meeting, it is worthwhile to organize the information according to general areas that comply with the IEP format. Bring notes sorted by these topics to stimulate discussion at the IEP meeting. List your questions for the team and for the parents. If the young person is present, come with some ideas for ways to help the child share areas where support is needed.

It is important to present the data as partial because more will be added at the formal IEP meeting. Certainly, staff team members want their input to be valued. In addition, parents want to know that this IEP is a living and breathing document in the making. They want the respect that their contributions will be considered and that the drafting of an individualized document is in fact that—an educational plan set up uniquely for one student from the perspectives and input of a team of which they are an integral part.

EDUCATIONAL

The clearest plans are those written for students with a learning disability or for those with speech issues. The instruction for these is specific and easy to explain. Plans for students on the autism spectrum or with emotional, social, behavioral, and functional issues may include solid academics, but in addition, include means for the student to learn alternative ways to behave in various environments. Sometimes those not familiar with special education might see these aspects of IEPs as less weighted in terms of content. However, drafting a plan to help a young person relearn behaviors, improve social function, and acquire ways to manage emotions is clearly important. Thus, all IEPs lend themselves to guiding the special education team in proper and personalized instruction.

Special educators focus on the individual needs of students and work to meet those needs. They assess where the student is functioning currently and what goals they want to establish to improve the skills of the student. They take into consideration student acquisition of curriculum, application of learned information, and the ability to function in a cross section of environments.

A student may know very well how to operate in a classroom setting, but a transition into a social environment may leave her ill-equipped. A student may comfortably function with parents in the home setting yet find it overwhelming to interact appropriately with peers during physical education, recess, science lab, or lunchtime. A student may be able to count imitation money in math class but be totally inept when trying to buy items in the school store or when going through a checkout line at a megastore.

Learning is an intricate experience of accessing, processing, retaining, and applying information. An IEP needs to reflect the big picture as it applies to qualifying areas of learning, behavior, social relationships, and functioning across environments.

PLAN

Those gathered at an IEP meeting plan goals and objectives for the student to assure progress and success based on the data gathered. They know that "one size doesn't fit all" and that the individual should be the primary focus. When taking this into consideration, the team considers appropriate methodologies, strategies, groupings, and situations that best meet the needs of the child.

Even if a child's entire class is being instructed in a whole-language type of reading program or a district-selected basal series, if a child needs a systematic phonics program with a controlled reading vocabulary to be successful, so be it. If a child needs a social situation where the special educator can help him build bridges with social contacts, that situation can be specified in the IEP plan.

Outside test results obtained by the parents need to be carefully considered. When parents have gone to this extent to learn why their child is struggling, they are serious about getting their son or daughter the appropriate help. Setting up an informal meeting with parents early in the process is wise. At that point, teachers and parents can forge a partnership, and when further school testing begins they can take the opportunity to compare and share information together. With this basis of respect and trust established, the parents will easily be able to merge into the staff team as significant contributing members.

As the team drafts goals and objectives, making them clear, measurable, and doable, those responsible for implementation begin to envision how to work this IEP plan into the existing school day. They consider students with similar needs and aim to schedule the new child with peers where the goals can be properly reinforced. The team looks at the whole picture. When does the child have lunch? How can pullout time be arranged so as not to impede optimal classroom learning or undercut supportive social opportunities?

Planning a student's school day is a significant decision. If done skill-fully, a student's schedule can support the child's academic and social success. If done poorly, all involved will struggle. For example, if a student with a visual memory deficit needs support in a social studies class, it would be better to remove the child from a room where he has good friends if the teacher is partial to a lecture-only style of presentation. Placing the child into a classroom where a special educator is already co-teaching with a social studies teacher who understands learning modalities and who provides visual and interactive dimensions to reinforce concepts would be well worth it. Finding another avenue for the student to be with his friends can be worked into the IEP by another means, and provision for this opportunity can be made informally.

The team must balance the big picture of the student's day with the detail of strategic instruction and measurement of success. Suppose a child with a learning disability and speech issues has difficulty with oral expression and language reception. This is a situation where there may be overlap between the domain of the LD teacher and the speech and language therapist. Perhaps these professionals can create an interactive group and work together with students on these skills, addressing and measuring various aspects of the child's needs under separate categories during the same session. Going at the child's needs from two different angles during a determined weekly time slot of twenty minutes is not only efficient but also a means of addressing the child's objectives effectively.

Teachers must use their time wisely. Perhaps a special educator has two students who eat lunch at the same time. Consider that one student has a social skills objective to initiate a conversation with a peer twice weekly during lunch and that the other has a functional objective to use correct eating utensils when spot-checked during the meal twice weekly. A special educator can tally results on both objectives during the same visit to the school cafeteria. Teachers who examine the objectives of students with an eye for developing big-picture and individualized plans are able to skillfully address student need in a workable and efficient manner.

Measurement of student progress is an important part of the IEP plan. If the IEP is too general in terms of reporting student success or difficulty, the team cannot accurately interpret whether a student has mastered an objective. On the other hand, if an objective tells where a student will be, how often the student is observed and measured, and what criterion is used to determine success, then all involved know the direction of the instruction and support designated for a student. When the team reviews the plan and data indicates where a student has been successful, objectives and benchmarks can be dropped, adjusted, or redone as the apparent need indicates.

No IEP plan is written in stone. Once a student demonstrates success according to the plan, new levels of measure can be included. This offers the entire team, including the parents and student, the concrete assurance that the effort to draft the plan, the work to attain the agreed-upon levels of performance, and the changes made in response to student progress have been well worth the time and energy expended. When a child reaches a benchmark of success, all agree it is due to the commitment of the group to teach and work according to an individualized educational plan.

APPLICATION OF IEP WRITING SKILLS
IN THE LIFE OF A SPECIAL EDUCATOR

The skills developed by a special educator in writing and implementing an IEP apply to the personal lives of a special educator. Certainly, were a teacher to have a child of his or her own or a relative with special needs, this teacher could be an excellent advocate for the child. In addition, she can apply her understanding of the IEP when family members become hospitalized or receive outside care.

To illustrate how a special educator uses skills related to the IEP process, let's consider two people we shall call Clare and Joe. Clare, an experienced special educator, chose to leave her job to support her husband, Joe, who showed signs of an undiagnosed neurological illness. Through several months and doctor appointments, Clare accompanied Joe, taking detailed notes, asking questions, and sharing her observations with medical personnel. She was a natural with record keeping, communicating, and coordinating information.

Ultimately, after several hospitalizations, Joe's doctor recommended that he move to a care center. When Clare met the staff, she automatically assumed that she was one of the team. Her comfort relating with past IEP teams was a perfect setup for her to merge with the care center team that not only included medical personnel but also a social worker as well as speech, occupational, and physical therapists.

When notified of Joe's first care conference, she organized topics of interest and her questions into categories such as medical, social, speech, occupational, and physical therapy. She came to the meeting with copies of a written agenda that she offered to all in attendance and provided not only input but also lent leadership in the discussion of Joe's needs.

When reviewing Joe's care plan periodically, Clare knows that the items on the plan are not merely a list of staff duties but an individualized plan of services that need to happen as stated for Joe's physical, social, and emotional benefit. If Clare notices that something on the plan has not been done, she calls this to the attention of the team. Since Clare has a special education background and is involved in the care of a family member, she can combine the roles of teacher and parent IEP team members to get things done on Joe's behalf.

Recently, Clare worked with the activity director at Joe's care center in supplying a project for a social work intern. With Joe's interests in mind, she helped them assemble a sensory basket of items that would be used to provide Joe with unique experiences through olfactory, auditory, and tactile means. She also included his resume and a joke so that the intern would have a basis for discussion with Joe about his life and interests. When told that the social work intern would be spending time with Joe three times per week for twenty minutes per session and that the intern would be recording what happened during her time with Joe, Clare knew that she was with professionals she could trust.

Clare learned from writing IEPs over many years that measurable goals and objectives, when followed consistently, bring growth. Consequently, she and her friend Helen meet monthly to share successes and challenges on their individual goals. Clare, being accustomed to goal categories, asks Helen to hold her accountable for spiritual, physical, emotional, personal, social, intellectual, recreational, and business objectives.

Having the background of working with IEPs helps Clare see the value of personal balance. Being a caregiver for her husband and a supporter for her mother, now in her nineties, Clare takes into account ways to assist both of these people who are important in her life. When she and Helen meet, they discuss a list of goals, not in a rigid manner, but with hearts intent on growing personally and helping those they care about as well.

SUMMARY

Skilled special educators individualize educational plans for students with special needs through detailed observation of the child and careful listening to staff and parents. They use their professional acumen to assemble content appropriate to the student and to design plans to meet their unique needs. In addition, special educators who have acquired solid experience writing effective IEPs prove to be helpful caregivers to family members with disabilities, those hospitalized and those living in care facilities, as they apply these individualized educational planning skills again and again.

Chapter Eight

The Ability to See
Progress in Small Steps

Melissa had been trained at a local state university. She found her classes very challenging and believed that the instructional concepts she learned would be helpful in her future as a teacher. What always struck her as unusual was the teaching style of her special education professors. Each one taught in a way that was very much in contrast to those instructors who taught core curriculum classes and electives. These classes were typically broad-brush lecture-style presentations. The professors in special education alternated their lectures with assigned presentations required of other students. In addition, these classes consisted of small-group exercises.

After being taught about the strategies that worked with the students she aimed to teach, Melissa began to analyze the teaching styles of her special education instructors. All three of the professors that had taught her education classes that semester had once been special education teachers themselves. Thus there was a common thread in their instructional strategies.

Each of these educators had given Melissa an "A." She mused that the "A" could have been due to her heightened interest in education as opposed to biology, for example. She considered that perhaps the education classes were easier for her than cultural anthropology or sociology. Closing her laptop after accessing her grade, Melissa began to mentally search for why she had done so well. Certainly she was looking forward to her future career. Would she have chosen teaching youth with special needs because it was an easier choice than going into engineering or medicine?

She was a bright young woman. She knew that from all the testing she had done in order to get into this institution. Why did some of her professors lose her attention in spite of this? What was the secret of success shared in common by Dr. Longman, Dr. Mallory, and Dr. Wooding? They were able to relate with their students. She just knew there was something about their instruction that connected with their past work experience. She now felt like a detective as she mentally reviewed class sessions and compared them based on her recent memory from the past semester.

Packing her laptop and heading to the student union, she walked across campus deep in thought. While passing in front of the oldest classroom building on campus, she heard someone call her name. "Melissa, are you solving the world's problems? What is with the intensity of expression there?" She looked up into the face of Robb Johansen, a classmate who had been with her in all three education classes as well as in her anthropology and sociology classes. He had teased her about feeing like she was being followed. On the first day of the semester, he continued to share classes with her, with the exception of those scheduled for Monday–Thursday at 9:45 a.m. There they parted ways, Melissa for anthropology and he for Spanish.

She laughed and then explained where her mind had wandered. Robb confessed to not having thought much about the question of professors' teaching styles but offered to think with her in the student union. When Melissa and Robb sat down they reviewed some of the personal habits of the teachers and even laughed at a few of their idiosyncrasies. Would Dr. Longman ever stop cleaning her glasses as she spoke? How about Dr. Mallory's constant use of the phrase "exceptions to every rule" or Dr. Wooding's apparent allergy to dust, which caused her to wrinkle her nose and sniff in the midst of a sentence?

Laughs aside, they got more serious and began digging around into the style of the class presentations. No fancy methods, no gimmicks—just solid learning. They reviewed and thought and hashed it all over. Then it occurred to them both at the same time. All three of these very down-to-earth yet skilled professors presented information in an ordered manner. Each concept presented was done in small, incremental steps.

Once it appeared that the group understood, these professors added another aspect or dimension to the educational concept. The reason for their success was that they practiced what they preached. In their words, they "broke the task or idea down into small steps." In doing so, students, even at the university level, were able to see and understand the inner workings of an idea when it was presented to them in pieces.

Both Robb and Melissa sat back and resolved from that moment that they too would approach lessons and life in the same manner. They realized that students in their future would need this in order to apply phonics for reading and spelling or to do a long division problem. So much of what they would be teaching could be presented one step at a time.

This solved, their topic switched to the new swing dancing class beginning the next semester. Both shared that they would be taking it and learned they would be doing so at the same time as well. Melissa laughed as Robb suggested that if they were partners and learned the dance steps one at a time, they would be able to put together a flawless program.

PRESENTING A FLAWLESS LESSON

Breaking a task down is essential and basic to teaching a lesson for children with special educational needs. (This strategy is explained in chapter 5 in the section "Reinforcing Successive Approximations: Looking for Progress in Small Steps.") Once a teacher has that strategy integrated into his or her repertoire, supporting student progress in smaller pieces becomes natural.

To back up and get behind any learned formal methods or any observed or acquired informal strategies that use the concept of breaking down a task, let us look inside the teacher. The special education teacher knows that the important part of doing a lesson in this manner is to have an affirming and encouraging attitude, supportive intentions, and an enduring presence. Accompanying effective and proven methodology with a peaceful and abiding presence ensures the student's success.

The teacher's purpose matters. A teacher may remember when she learned to ride a bicycle and her father held on to her seat to make sure she rode with steadiness and felt secure. As the father sensed that the steadiness and security increased in the child, he carefully and gradually let up on his hold on the bike. Back and forth, he held on and let go, held on and let go, offering his daughter words of encouragement. As she was becoming more and more sure of herself as a cyclist, he was easing up more and more on his part of the process. Due to the combination of his skill, care, and intuition, he knew when to release his daughter to ride freely and joyfully by herself.

The same is true for teachers. They come to a lesson with concern, expertise, and intuition. They know how much to present, how much to support, and when to let the students go forward on their own. Certainly the father knew how to ride a bike, but there is much more to teaching someone else than that, as has been described. The same is true for the special education teacher. University training and understanding of the best theories and practices is only part of the process. The manner, attitude, and persona of the teacher make for a fully successful imparting of skills and information.

If a student were learning to make lemon bars in a family and consumer science class, a successful teacher and students would need to begin with assembling the ingredients and then following a sequence of actions, the recipe, in order to complete the task of creating this delicious snack. This is a concrete means of working in steps that yields a natural reward—the opportunity to eat the lemon bars and share them with enthusiastic classmates.

Yet no matter what the concept being taught, a skilled special educator will find a way to not only break down the task for student understanding and success but also to make sure that the students understand they are successful. There is more to a reward than eating a lemon bar, or two or three! Once students really believe the teacher's message that a performance is great, the task is correct, and that learning will be applicable in the future, then they have really been rewarded with the sense of knowing their capabilities.

They are independent with a skill or information. They know they are now successful because their special education teacher knew them uniquely, knew how much information to present—not too little so that they feel the teacher does not believe in them, but also not too much so that they do not feel overwhelmed and get discouraged. Again, the teacher certainly knows the methodology but has also acquired the art of knowing how to impart knowledge so that it matches the student. This match is created through correct language that they "get"—the right timing and the right objects, images, and sensory components. When a teacher does this, the lesson is truly flawless and the school environment becomes a place of honor and joy for all students.

Breaking a task down into smaller steps applies in the school environment, but it also allows educators to relate and engage with others who have educational and physical needs requiring support, not only in their classroom but also in other relationships and in the broader community. Because special educators have developed the ability to break concepts down into small steps, they automatically transfer this skill to social relationships: student-to-student, student-to-teacher, teacher-to-teacher, and teacher-to-family and friends. They also apply this skill as individuals in terms of their self-acceptance, self-care, and in working with small groups.

IN RELATIONSHIPS

Teaching social skills works well when an action is broken down and reviewed. Teachers also break down processes when speaking one to another. Imagine a teacher going into the classroom next door after school and asking another teacher how to get to the baby shower being held for the new special education paraprofessional. The reply will be much clearer than something like "go down Bluff Street near the hardware store and you will see our cars." Instead, this teacher may even grab a pencil and list the direction steps one at a time, reviewing and checking as she goes to ensure that her colleague has the right information. Such directions may even be clarified by drawing a map.

As another example, imagine two teachers having coffee in the lounge after school and one wants to know how to use a certain feature when projecting a lesson by computer. Again, the person asked will pause to consider how best to explain the process so that the colleague needing assistance will be successful. And since the computer is not in the lounge, the teacher may grab a napkin or pull out a pad of paper and slowly and deliberately impart information to the teacher seeking the explanation. This teacher for sure will treasure that napkin or scrap of paper through the solo trial run back in his classroom.

Special educators do not abandon their minds, mannerisms, and way of relating once they are with their families. For instance, when a teacher arrives at home and finds her son unsure of how to use the microwave for making popcorn, the teacher-mom, with emphasis on the numbers, says the following: "One: open the door. (pause) Two: place the bag inside the microwave, making sure it is flat. (pause) Three: close the door. (pause) Four: set the time for two minutes and thirty seconds. (pause) Five: push the "start" button. Amidst his assertions that he knows how to open and close a microwave door, teacher-mom may even decide to join her son for popcorn, telling him what a great job he did making this healthy snack.

That same evening, the same teacher-mom, when getting together with her own mother at a local yarn shop to knit, will have the occasion to offer her parent some help with a pattern. In this circumstance, she would read the challenging section over first, breaking the task down so that her mother will see where to insert the needle. Once her mom is in position, she shows her how to move her yarn under the needle to start to create the unique stitch described in the pattern. After that she will talk her through completion of the stitch. Thus sitting side-by-side, teacher-daughter and her mother begin, one step at a time, to create the specified unique design with needles and yarn.

This teacher has a lot going on outside of her school world. Not only does she assist her family but she also comes across clearly when with friends by presenting her ideas and information to them incrementally. When weight training with her exercise partner, this special educator demonstrates how to lift in the hammer-curl style using alternate arms. Asking her friend to stand beside her with both of them facing a full-length, wall-sized mirror, the teacher asks her friend to assume a certain posture, hold the ten-pound weights with a particular grip, and then demonstrates the alternate arm movements. Her friend feels capable because this special educator made this easy by teaching it to her in steps. The entire training was not done in one complete action but in such a way that her friend could safely assume the correct position, hold the weights correctly, and alternate arms in the right way.

When someone in the field has the opportunity to assist an adult family member with any of a variety of complex neurological conditions, it comes naturally. For example, in order to offer support for a basic household task such as doing laundry, one could break down the options offered with so many buttons on the machine. By putting colored dots at points on the washer/dryer, selections of only the necessary options become apparent. Thus the person can follow fewer steps in the process.

Making the transfer from a wheelchair to a car is a multistep process. Again, someone in special education would value an automobile with a handle positioned to assist the person making the transition into the passenger seat. By first giving the cue to grip the handle with the right hand, then directing the person to move the left foot onto the mat, helping the individual slide onto the seat makes this a doable operation.

When working with home care aides, a special educator moves into the teacher/paraprofessional relationship and thinks of ways to offer direction. When the family member is gone, the aide benefits from step-by-step suggestions of what to do with the person in various situations. Following is an example of written instructions.

1. When assisting with a meal, it works best to sit left of Mom as she is left-handed.
2. Then put the specially modified cup to the left of her.
3. She does best when you put the same type of foods on the plate in the same spot.
4. After the meal, assist Mom in leaving the kitchen and supporting her as she sits down to watch TV.

In addition, the teacher would leave a checklist of jobs to complete while the person is napping, ranking them in order of priority. Doing this for a home care aide helps offer focus and maximizes the use of the aide's time. Organizing tasks in steps in this fashion enhances communication. These types of supportive interventions would be typical of any special educator.

IN THE BROADER COMMUNITY

When special educators get involved in projects beyond school, community members appreciate them certainly for stepping up, but also for the quality they bring to the involvement. Suppose a secondary special education teacher was elected to chair a civic project that included assembling holiday food packages to be distributed to those who are in need. He first showed his skill of breaking down a task by explaining to volunteers how to assemble gift boxes.

He gave each team a list of items and the order of placing them into the holiday bags so that the heavier items were at the bottom and the more breakable or lighter ones were visible and secure at the top. Before asking each team to fill a bag, he demonstrated first, reading each item off the list and showing how to fit them together so that each was well-placed in the bag. After this, he gave each team a map of the city. He had clearly broken the city into parts, assigning one per team, so that delivery would be easier, faster, and more efficient.

When a special education teacher helps clean up the side of the road for a summer church youth group outing, she supports the other adult leaders by bringing clarity and purpose to the task. Instead of handing the young people bags and expecting them to pick up items scattered at the roadside, she divides the young people into small groups. She then suggests that one team of young people keep an eye out for bottles and collect them while another team looks for paper and places that in their bag. As these teams work, another team is asked to collect cans and places them in their common bag. Then another team follows behind, assigned to collect general garbage. Not only has the teacher given order and focus to the mission but she has also set up the bags for direct recycling.

IN THE INDIVIDUAL TEACHER

Special educators use their skills of breaking down tasks when they are alone in an effort to solve problems in their personal lives. For instance, when having a goal to declutter an apartment, a teacher, instead of randomly grabbing items here and there, might make a list of the rooms and then assign a certain amount of time per day or per week to work on the room. This could be as short as five minutes. The smaller the expectation, the more likely something will get done. The teacher may begin in one corner and systematically go from drawer to drawer, table to table, extracting items to be boxed or bagged for pickup by a charity organization, setting aside unusable items for the trash during the process.

Maybe a teacher for children with special needs will kick into her instructional mode when planning time for personal reading. Having a novel the local library procured from another system with a limited time allowed for completion, she may check the number of chapters or pages and determine how many a day she will have to read in order to finish the book on time.

An organization that dedicates itself to the development of the skill of public speaking is Toastmasters International. Special educators are among the members who benefit from developing their speaking ability. In a recent issue of the *Toastmasters* magazine (2008), a contributing writer, Richard

Bonner, suggested using the incremental approach to improving speaking. He stated the following:

> Let's realize that the commitment and effort needed to excel in speaking seem far less unnerving if we demand only small but continuous steps of improvement from ourselves. This incremental approach takes major pressure off us yet puts improvement on a comfortable auto-pilot. Then one day, without our feeling the pain of the process, it just dawns on us that we've become darned good speakers (p. 13).

Educators who break down tasks for themselves, whether the improvement of speaking, decluttering an apartment, or completing a book on time, find satisfaction and success when they chip away at the process one step at a time.

STEPS TO SELF-ACCEPTANCE

Self-acceptance is an ongoing process and does not occur overnight. It is not unusual for teachers to work with students as they try and try again to gain mastery over a challenging academic task. In such circumstances, teachers not only help students break down a task but also offer them ways to think about their performance at each step in both academic and social situations. When doing so the teacher's demonstration and the teacher's words become incorporated into the student's thinking. The introduction of the teacher's manner of solving a problem one way or a way of thinking makes a solid inroad into the minds of students.

In the same manner, special educators who struggle with a lesson or a relationship at work or in a personal context may monitor their thoughts when self-acceptance is waning due to frustration. Maybe a computer program is hard to learn when one is trying to assist a student in a general education class. A teacher may feel uncomfortable in front of the general education teacher who is a master at this particular lesson. Not only must the special educator get up-to-speed with the lesson but also demonstrate to the student how to do it. This is when ready self-talk comes in handy for the special education teacher. Prepared affirmation, in three simple steps, may help. Following is a suggestion to have on hand.

1. I am a competent and well-trained special educator.
2. When I meet a challenge I take a deep breath and do my best to address it.
3. I am okay with asking for help from coworkers.

Just like students, teachers also run into social difficulties both on the job and in other settings. No two people are ever in the exact same place in their life's journey. Sometimes coworkers or other adults in various relationships are focused on a certain aspect of life that conflicts with another. Each individual holds a different viewpoint based upon a variety of things such as age, gender, time of day, circumstances from the past, or something that has happened a few minutes before a conversation begins.

When things do not start off on the right foot for a student in a social situation, the teacher might tell her that people care about her, that she can try again, or that other relationships may work better for her and to move on. To affirm self-acceptance, a teacher can do this type of on-the-spot evaluation when coming up against a disagreeable colleague, a disappointed parent, or a friend who seems distant. By stepping back and considering the following, a special education professional can hold firm on self-acceptance. The following is a sample set of affirmations.

1. This person may be having a difficult day or time in life.
2. I do my best and sometimes this does not always meet another's expectations.
3. I speak with sincerity, honesty, and respect to all.
4. If we cannot work things out, I will bring in a third party or move on.

Certainly teachers cannot move on from parents and coworkers. However, they can move on from their own attitudes about their relationships with these individuals and cut themselves some slack. Holding on to self-acceptance under pressure gives them more leverage to redeem a potentially broken relationship or situation of conflict.

Training the attitude, by breaking a situation down, is a natural thing for teachers to do for their students. Consequently, special education teachers are naturals for maintaining self-acceptance for themselves through challenging school and personal encounters. The more self-acceptance is tested, the more special educators know in their heart of hearts that they are worthwhile, capable, and have much to offer students and other individuals they meet on the journey of life.

STEPS TO SELF-CARE

Another aspect where special education teachers seek to improve themselves is in self-care. For them, eating correctly would be essential in order to do the job with adequate energy and alertness. Even planning healthy meals for the week so as to pack lunches that limit fattening and cholesterol-causing foods works well. Arranging the refrigerator so that they can pull out a range of food in order allows teachers to cover their bases to include a variety of healthy foods quickly and efficiently.

If one wants to ensure the inclusion of eight glasses of water a day, one could find a large jug and mark it at levels to indicate each eight-ounce glass of water. Thus, a large jug of water can be perceived as divided into eight parts, the total daily requirement broken down into doable portions.

Sleep is something that everyone in the field needs for sure. Yet getting to sleep is not always easy, as much detail fills the mind. Thus the "task of sleep" is also something to break down. Perhaps one could ease into this as early as dinnertime. Eating a slow and relaxed meal sends the signal to the body to wind down. Follow this by reading a book with a pleasant theme, then taking a hot bubble bath or sitting in a hot tub, steam room, or sauna at a fitness club. Later, put on comfortable loungewear and turn on soothing sounds on a classical station or a CD of nature sounds. Spend some time with spirituality, such as thoughts of gratitude for the gifts of the day, pushing out any work-related anger or anxiety-producing images. Ease into bed. Breathe as if sleep had already begun. Soon the real thing, the last step, sleep, arrives for the night, assuring a restful entry into tomorrow.

A suggestion offered by Bahram Akradi (2008), founder and CEO of Lifetime Fitness, would work well for a special educator aiming to incrementally increase exercise and succeed step-by-step with other personal endeavors. Though he recommends "ambitious and expansive ... goals," he believes it is important to break off a bit at a time. Akradi shares the following:

> "Start Small" saves me from getting overwhelmed by what I've taken on and lets me get started *now* with modest daily actions that feel doable. Daily action equates with integrity and determination, in my view. You have to keep asking yourself: Do I really want this thing or not? Each day brings the opportunity to reconfirm your priorities and to move forward by doing *something*. Even if the action is just a single phone call, a few breaths on the yoga mat, or a swift left turn out of the snack aisles, it's still a step in the right direction and it builds momentum for more positive action (p. 10).

Special educators find unlimited ways to save time, organize their lives, and improve a skill just because they know how to break down a task. Our advantage is that we do this automatically more often than we realize.

IN SMALL GROUPS

We stop to consider a task and determine how to break it down when doing small group work at staff meetings, in graduate and in-service classes, and in committee gatherings. For example, when someone presents a goal, offers a description of the end of a project, puts out a vision, or gives an assignment, we, as special educators, aim for that end. We know that we cannot wait until the night before a project is due to work on it. Who wants to panic and stay up until 5:00 a.m. anyway? Thus, we make suggestions or join in with the plans of others that involve tackling the project in parts. Maybe we get out the calendar and decide how long each part of the project will take. We ask that as a team we hold one another accountable for making each ministep along the way. If the group is behind, we prod our team along. We encourage, we motivate, we ask for the same from them to ensure that we are on track as well.

If we have a separate contribution assigned to us, we lay out the project in pieces and put them in order. After that we look at our calendar, schedule in an hour or two here and there to work at each segment. We set a timer and focus for the allotted time. When the timer alerts us that we are formally finished, we evaluate if we are on track or not. If we are, it's time to go to the health club, have a snack break, or watch TV. If we are not on time, we do a little more and adjust all of the future allotments of time accordingly.

When we reach the completion of the project, we are pleased, proud, and perfectly relaxed. We have completed an admirable work, stayed steadily with the task, and done the job on time. This is what students learn from special educators who teach and model working at sections.

MAKING MOUNTAINS DOABLE

Often tasks seem like mountains to students serviced by special education staff. Likewise, projects that staff members undertake, such as writing lesson plans, working on a master's degree, or maintaining a personal wellness program appear as mountains as well. Everything is relative.

Peter DeLeo (2005) wrote of his challenging experience after his single-engine Maule plane crashed in the Sierra Nevada. Leaving two other passengers behind with the plane, he spent thirteen days in subfreezing temperatures with broken bones, hiking in search of help for the trio. When he encountered a mountain, DeLeo looked ahead, determined points to aim toward, such as rocks or trees, and concentrated on scaling just one part of a mountain at a time.

He took into consideration the location of the sun and how long it would take for him to reach a predetermined point. Then he gauged himself accordingly. This made each mountain less daunting for him. When on a road near the end of his wanderings, he deliberately looked down in order to focus only on a segment of his journey. Having the mind-set of aiming for rescue, traveling one step at a time enabled him to make it out of dangerous terrain alive.

When working with students, it is important for them to learn how to take steps toward their own "mountains," whether in the form of curricular or social challenges. They, like DeLeo, can also reach their destination. Special educators who stay the course, break tasks into doable fragments, and remain steadfast, self-affirming, and determined will traverse their professional and personal "mountains." When doing so, special educators are capable of bringing their students, parents, coworkers, family, and friends with them to further growth and success.

SUMMARY

Special educators work successfully with students when they break a learning task down into small steps. In addition to using this technique when teaching, a special educator enhances the process by using intuition, affirmation, and support when guiding a student toward further knowledge.

This approach to instruction automatically transfers to social relationships between students, a student and teacher, among teachers and with parents, family, and friends. Using their honed ability to break concepts down into smaller sections, special educators naturally apply this strategy to self-acceptance, self-care, and working with small groups.

REFERENCES

Akradi, B. (2008). Think big, step lightly. *Experience Life 9(3), (April)*, 10.
Bonner, R. (2008). Opt to be an outstanding orator. *Toastmaster, 74(9)*, 13.
DeLeo, P. (2005). *Survive!* New York: Simon & Schuster.

Chapter Nine

The Ability to Adapt

Bridget and Virginia taught special education at Lone Valley Elementary for what seemed like forever. Actually, they had worked there together for ten years. As a team they maintained a sterling reputation for caring for their students and assisting families. One day Virginia casually mentioned that she had been at Lone Valley for too long and thought maybe she should consider making some changes in her career. This came as a real shock to Bridget, who had always seen her colleague and good friend as someone who was very stationary, structured, and orderly.

That evening, when Bridget sat in traffic on her way to her downtown loft apartment, she mused on what Virginia had said. She knew her friend, whom she called Ginna, was able to be adaptable with students, but she never appeared to seek out change in her own life. As her cranberry compact moved between seven and twenty-three mph, she recalled how Ginna supported Matt, a student with behavioral issues and ADHD, in a general education classroom during his social studies period.

Ginna naturally noticed when Matt needed order, as the teacher typically ran her class in a very unpredictable and scattered fashion. Ginna made him a plan for the expected sequence of events in the class to counter the teacher's random style. She based this on a quick and informal preclass interview done with the teacher in the hall. When Matt knew what to expect he had a better chance of remaining calm for the hour. Also, when the teacher tended to veer off topic and rattle on, Ginna pulled out the main points of the lesson and formulated the concept for Matt. She did this by not only listing the ideas but also by drawing out a visual explanation so that he could stay on topic and understand the concept.

When a new student, Katie, transferred to Lone Valley from another school district, Ginna picked up on her deficits immediately. Though there were some accommodations noted on Katie's IEP, Ginna went beyond that and incorporated additional adaptations to assist Katie. For example, when Katie struggled with reading from left to right on a page, Ginna immediately grabbed her own scissors and a piece of bright tag board from the scrap box to create a marker. This helped the new girl focus on her place in the story.

On Katie's first day she randomly tossed her coat into the closet. Ginna again grabbed her scissors and took a roll of tape from her drawer, labeling a hook for the new student. This astute teacher correctly predicted the girl's need for organizational assistance by making her a personal daily schedule and helping her arrange her desk for maximum efficiency.

By now Bridget was again stalled at a complete stop, as there had been an accident ahead. She found herself focused on one of the many bumper stickers pasted on the car ahead of her. A graphic of a tilted palm tree accompanied a phrase that corresponded with her thoughts. It read, "As far as adaptability goes, palm trees get it." Funny she should spot that one. It made her think about her own life and the ways she had made accommodations outside of school.

Bridget's Irish grandmother had died only recently. When she and her mom had visited her in the past, Bridget, as a special education person, instinctively noticed her grandmother's needs. One day Bridget observed her grandmother, with the aid of a walker, stop directly beneath the kitchen clock and stretch her neck in order to tell the time. That was Bridget's clue to buy her a new clock with large numbers for her St. Patrick's Day birthday.

Bridget, still at a complete stop, then reviewed the stage of visiting her in the care center. After her grandmother's stroke, she became anxious because she could not always remember the anticipated date of their next visit. Bridget saw this need and bought her grandmother a white board, placing it in a prominent place in her tiny room. On it she listed the date and time visitors would be coming. This way her grandmother not only felt calmer but could also experience growing anticipation for these visits, because she knew who to expect and when to expect them.

Now that Bridget was feeling a sense of satisfaction about her own skills, the cars began to move. She pushed the accelerator of her small car and moved with the traffic between fifty-five and sixty mph. She was anxious to get home, but more eager to hurry to school tomorrow. Her main thought was "What was up with Ginna? Career change? A move?" Her curiosity was growing as she drove into her underground parking space.

The next day, Bridget wasted no time posing the question about Ginna's interest in change. Her coworker explained that she had decided to satisfy her slowly growing yen for adventure and spent the evening online looking for options. She tossed a stack of downloaded papers about teaching overseas onto

Bridget's desk. Bridget was stunned. But she was more surprised when Ginna pulled out a list of countries and said, "Where should *we* teach next year?"

Bridget looked at a vertical list of countries, each with the first letter highlighted in hot pink. Ginna had written them in a certain order to make a point. Bridget got the message loud and clear when she saw **A**rgentina, **D**enmark, **A**ustralia, **P**eru, and **T**ogo. Certainly she could see the acronym—ADAPT!

Together they began talking about their experience at Lone Valley and came to the conclusion that it might be time to move out of the valley toward new horizons. Their skills as special educators would travel with them to a new setting and possibly even assist them in adapting to a new culture.

THE ART OF ADAPTABILITY

Being an adaptable person can be a challenge. Certainly special educators have to be ready for unforeseen events at any time. Actually, anyone working in education continuously accommodates students, parents, and staff as they keep up with constant changes in curriculum, personnel, and methodology.

Education staff face endless challenges. Nevertheless, educators are up to the task. McGrath (1995) presents a vision for educational adaptability, describing this art as an array of options:

> Once one has loosened the mind and attitude with flexibility and openness, one will be able to move into any unknown situation, setting, work expectation, or challenge with an adaptability that will empower one to succeed. It does not mean hiding in the security of tenure and riding it out to retirement, but being willing to create the vision of our own professional futures. Being adaptable may mean specifically working cooperatively as part of a team, respecting one another's philosophies, differences, styles, and strengths. It could mean coping with downsizing as is done in business, and being able to assume new roles. For some, it will mean being willing to go through whatever may seem like constant training to be prepared for whatever is required. Administrators need to consider ways to free their staff for this retooling, such as giving them opportunities to attend conventions, visit other educational sites and maintain association with educators in their particular disciplines. It may mean moving over to accommodate the talents and offerings of coworkers or being able to step into new paradigms that arise in response to an ever-changing future world. It might mean being a pathfinder, ever willing to work any situation to the optimal advantage of expressed student needs. It may mean surrendering our individual hold on fragmented and territorial work settings for more integrated, whole and cooperative settings (p. 113).

When a teaching professional makes the decision to be adaptable, this choice brings about broad-ranging effects. Not only does this choice affect students but it can also potentially change the entire atmosphere of a school. Once teachers collectively work to accommodate their students, families, and colleagues, they tap into the capability of changing the culture not only of a building but also of education as a whole.

Broad and long-range positive changes in education start within the heart and mind of the individual educator. Some environments are improved when a new person enters the group, and others can decline as a result of the presence of one single teacher, administrator, paraprofessional, or support staff member.

Typically, special education personnel work within small groupings. It is there that they artfully put into place accommodations so that their students succeed. It is also there that they make significant connections with one another. From this solid base they build bridges to the broader school community. Receptivity to what these groups of specialists have to offer to general education on behalf of their students is determined by how adaptable they are when working with their generalist colleagues.

Anyone who has taught special education has been required to work in a variety of settings, programs, or alternative environments within a particular school. They have done so when accompanying students to a variety of classes and activities, teaming with teachers adept at various academic subjects, and working in tandem with parents for the benefit of youth.

Not only does the art of adaptability involve helping students through supportive enhancement of strengths and devising accommodations for deficit areas but also artfully adapting when they move from school to home to community. Special educators remain in tune with their ability to use accommodations when traveling, when dealing with a variety of adult personalities, and in meeting the everyday challenges of life.

MOVING FROM SCHOOL, TO HOME, TO THE COMMUNITY

When special educators come back to their home turf after a school day, they arrive complete with their professional training, instincts, and responses. These aspects of their full personality remain in effect while at home and when out in the community. This means they hold solid when interacting with their own families.

Manhattan, New York, special educator Mary Donovan explains how her training has helped her adapt to raising a teenager. "Just today my 17 year old daughter demanded $$$$$$ for a weekend visit. I told her that she was too rude and had to approach me in a more reasonable manner. Just maybe 2 years ago I probably might have opened up my wallet just to get her out of the room and to end the conflict" (M. Donovan, email interview with author, January 15, 2009). Mary was no more going to buckle in the face of a teen demand in her home than she would have at school. Skilled in adapting to the varied moods of teens, Mary remained steady as a matter of course.

When special educators move into the role of parent, they model skills developed for dealing with challenging behavior. Casper, Wyoming, special education teacher Laurie Fedje shares how her son has adopted and applied her skills.

> My son was raised around many of our special families and I didn't realize the skills and awareness he picked up. Just one example: When in Denver 3 years ago James was in a deli where a stressed out street person (vet) was freaking out, ranting, and was beside himself. James went to him and said, "Hey! You are scaring all the big people here. Come sit with me for a little while and I'll give you a dollar." The man did come sit with him, calmed down and was able to go on his way. James gauged the level of threat and was able to connect with this man. My friends who were there said they felt someone without the skills to gauge threat and intervene would probably have gotten hurt. Because of my work James has developed into an adult who is a natural advocate for people who have special needs (L. Fedje, email interview with author, January 16, 2009).

In a sense, as with other mannerisms, children of special educators inherit abilities to serve the common good in unique and supportive ways.

Academic training comes in handy just as it is. Often teachers assist their family members with subject matter, much to the benefit of the young person and certainly to the satisfaction of the adult educator. Mary Donovan asserts that this has been a theme in her life for quite awhile. "Yes, I use a lot of my training at home with my daughter Alice who is 13 and has had learning difficulties since kindergarten. I know how to structure her homework, sometimes even with a timer. I give her rewards for finishing and while she is working I cut down on as many distractions as I can" (M. Donovan, email interview with author, January 14, 2009). Good teaching involves knowing content and how to individually adapt it, setting up the right conditions and reinforcing effort.

Whether at home or in the community, a teacher's manner, demeanor, and wherewithal manifest themselves as automatic assets. For instance, when attending a community meeting or serving on a board, the special educator communicates completely with explanatory hand gestures that assist students in getting the point of an explanation. A special educator makes impact by use of voice tone for emphasis, eye contact for connection, and posture for projection of confidence in an idea or opinion.

Other school skills automatically transfer into the public arena as they serve others. Again, Mary Donovan explains. "I often end up on committees at church and in my women's clubs. This is because I have learned to be organized at school and I can set goals; this is what I do all the time with annual reviews!" (M. Donovan, email interview with author, January 14, 2009). What is required at school comes naturally elsewhere.

Laurie Fedje also brings her classroom skills to her church community, providing them support with children's classes. She describes how she has supplied these youth with structure and brought in academic skills as follows:

> These classes usually struggle with some students who are disrespectful and non-compliant. Setting up rules, consequences, and ways for adults to teach these expectations make the classes much easier to maintain. I have also shown the adults ways to supplement with materials for students who have special needs or have difficulty reading text. I have used these same skills to help families use structure at home to keep children busy and out of trouble. What we used to call "hand work" years ago (knitting, drawing, sewing, painting) might include building with Legos or other connex toys today. These skills are both calming and therapeutic. We sometimes find them to be simple answers to behavior problems (L. Fedje, email interview, January 16, 2009).

To those outside the field, these school skills are valued qualities. Special educators might do well to pause and realize how their many gifts are admired and valued when adapted for various organizations.

ADAPTING WHEN TRAVELING

Teachers are known to love traveling. Many take advantage of time off in the summer and at holidays for this purpose. Yet, is this opening in their schedule the main reason special educators travel, or is there another reason?

Traveling involves continuous change and adaption to environments and people. This is exactly what special educators do at work, at home, and in the community. Would they be drawn to travel because they are comfortable and capable when it comes to being adaptable?

A special education teacher who travels to a contrasting culture will likely have prepared to reduce surprises. When in another city, country, or continent, the special education professional becomes inventive—creative about how to see the sights, how to organize the days of the trip, and how to experience multiple facets of a new place.

When on a tour they know how to read the group, and having that skill, select those companions they believe they can best team up with in order to enjoy the free time available.

The special educator listens, takes organized notes, and captures the essence of the experience in a journal and when writing postcards. They know how to access information in preparation for travel and how to integrate their learning to enhance their experiences.

Special educators sometimes take bold steps and choose to teach outside their own countries. When they do, they rely on their skills and strength. They also learn to creatively cope with new and unique challenges. Bloomington, Minnesota, public schools' special education teacher, Chris Reano, is one such person. When teaching in Uganda, Chris applied her ability to adapt as she brought benefit to her students. She describes an experience quite different from what she had at her public school.

When I was in Uganda, I had anywhere from 60–80+ high school students in a room that would have comfortably fit 40 or so; with roughly made wooden benches, on which 3–5 students would squeeze themselves. Some had notebooks, some had pencils, some had pens; often they "shared" materials. My materials were one old English book, chalk and a horrific chalkboard. The windows were many and wide open; the roof a tin sheet. Bat droppings from the rafters, birds and the occasional chicken coming in were not unusual distractions. When the rain came, the sound of it on the roof drowned out any other sound (i.e., my teaching).

Student attendance fluctuated constantly. During planting and harvesting times of the year, students were needed at home to work; also, the AIDS situation in Africa being what it is meant that many families were caring for multiple sick people and so often students were put in the position of being caretaker for the sick, or the caretaker of the babies and younger siblings, again putting school on the back burner.

So, how did I teach? Good question! A Day at a Time. I learned a lot about just what I could control; and SO MUCH about what I couldn't control!

I ended up copying things out of the book I had, onto the board, the kids then dutifully copied it in their notebooks. If there was reading to be done, I read aloud to the group. Discussions of any kind were nearly impossible . . . Now that I think about it, I really don't know how I did it! (C. Reano email interview, January 27, 2009).

The key is that Chris did do it. When in a different environment, special educators open themselves to challenges at hand and adapt. Whether far from the familiar, or when traveling with students to alternate environments within their own schools, they modify as circumstances dictate.

Special education teachers not only know how to maximize their time of travel for themselves but also for others, especially for family members. Mary Donovan explains how she prepares for travel and also brings an added dimension to the experience for her daughters. "I always plan ahead for what

I am going to do, and plan things for my children, even on the airplane. We will decide on a card game or some activities before we leave home—like lesson plans for school!!!!" (M. Donovan, email interview with author, January 14, 2009).

When a special education teacher vacations with a family member with a disability, a significant success is that the teacher believes it is even possible for them to venture out. The special educator is not afraid to plan ahead, taking into consideration any adaptations needed for the person in the family with special needs. The teacher easily anticipates potential challenges and in advance determines ways to meet them. The special educator, if necessary, hires help and either brings assistants along or arranges to meet them at the destination location. These specially trained teachers arrange for a disability-adapted hotel room. They call the airlines explaining transfer and dietary needs. They arrange for transport to a hotel that accommodates those with special needs.

If the individual needing support takes medication, the family expert arranges them in the hotel room just as they are at home. If the individual does special speech or physical therapy exercises, a family member or accompanying aide helps with them. When the group arrives, they immediately fall into a routine so that they all know what to expect.

Mainly, special education teachers show the willingness to not only see possibilities at home but also help shape the lives of relatives with disabilities so they can see possibilities as well. It seems special education staff are wired to not only find growth in travel for themselves but for others as well. They are alert to nuances in a setting, possibilities for what to see and who to approach. They use their instincts to remain safe and pace themselves in balance so they can enjoy their time away.

DEALING WITH A RANGE OF PERSONALITIES IN PUBLIC

Special educators spend hours each year with young people who have a difficult time managing angry feelings and show fluidity of emotions, work slowly on tasks, become manipulative, fixate on a single idea or object, and have good intelligence along with deficits. These students will become adults in due course. Special educators recognize these qualities when engaged with adults in their daily lives. When they do have such encounters, they know exactly how to respond.

For instance, Mary Donovan tells how she has grown in dealing with anger in others due to her work experience. She states that, "Since I have learned how to deal with angry outbursts from students, I don't panic quite as much when I get an angry reaction from one of my children or outside my home. I can distance myself and then do something once I 'catch a breath'" (M. Donovan, email interview, January 14, 2009).

Laurie Fedje (2009) recounts that most of her "experiences which draw on special ed training concern helping others deal with emotional and behavioral outbursts (at church, in the grocery store, on the street, at the public library where homeless people tend to gather)." She tells about a time she spontaneously intervened at a social service agency because a woman became aggressive toward staff.

> She felt they were not helping her in the way she needed. The staff replied by telling her to move on, which caused her to escalate and become physically threatening toward them. I did step in and ask the staff if they could wait a moment so I could talk to this lady. The woman let me step in so I told her "If we kill them all they will never get this paperwork done. What do you think would be best?" The woman laughed, then cried, calmed down and visited with me in a corner for a few minutes about her frustrations. I helped her get another appointment with the correct person. She gave me a hug on her way out. Humor and a little kindness can mean all the difference. Special ed. training has helped me develop heightened awareness of people's emotional limits and the ability to offer a quick bit of help to prevent problems. Life seems so stressful today. Many people are strained to the limit and can easily go over the edge (L. Fedje, email interview, January 16, 2009).

Laurie has also drawn upon her skills in dealing with adults who show emotional fluidity and become manipulative. For background she shares that her "husband often teaches Bible studies. Some of the people who attend have had very dysfunctional lives and are very good at 'using' other people. Some feel entitled to be verbally abusive. Some seem low functioning due to years of alcohol or chemical abuse. My husband is very adept at dealing with them."

Each spouse in this situation employs their own style of relating to these individuals. Laurie draws upon her proven special education skills. She shares how she handled the same situation.

> I myself had to draw upon my skills in establishing boundaries to protect myself. I give specific examples of how people can get my attention and which behaviors would definitely NOT get my attention. "I will consider you out of bounds when you use gross profanity or sexually explicit language. If you try to get me to take care of you or your responsibilities, I will consider you out of bounds. Stay in bounds and I will be there for you." In the beginning I specifically tell people when they are out of bounds. Time, repetition, and relationship often (but not always) do the trick. Respect for boundaries is an essential skill for any adult (L. Fedje, email interview, January 16, 2009).

The key to dealing with people whose emotions run all over the map is to be with them in that feeling place, but not to act as they do. Mary Donovan says that due to her training she "can stay even when others are melting from one emotion to another" (M. Donovan, email interview, January 14, 2009). In the presence of a properly trained, stable, serene, and mature adult, those who tend to lose control of their emotions or express them inappropriately can come back onto solid ground.

RISING TO THE OCCASION IN SITUATIONS REQUIRING EMOTIONAL AND PHYSICAL FLEXIBILITY

When teachers of children of special needs find themselves in a situation where they are caring for a vulnerable adult, whether through gradual decline or sudden onset of an illness, they reach into their skill base. There they find several options readily available from continuous use on the job. Even when retired, teachers discover that their inclinations to assist others in a particular way come to the fore.

When caregivers support someone who lives at home, they look for ways to make the environment more accessible. When they make these accommodations in school, they may not always know how to apply them to adult situations. However, they do know that parallel models and means are there. Thus they seek out and listen to those who regularly work at making accommodations for adults with special needs living with support at home. Following are five ways to create an adapted home:

1. *Ease access.* If a person moves about with the assistance of a walker or uses a wheelchair, getting in and out of the home can sometimes be very difficult. Adding a ramp at one access point serves to ease the transition in and out of the house. When assisting someone needing to be transferred in and out of a car, using cues, a grab bar, and a transfer belt increase success. Putting railings in and outside the home allows access to a room that would be off limits without them.
2. *Install safety measures.* Grab bars placed at strategic spots support independence with a function or at least less difficultly in doing something like taking a shower. Adding a shower chair and flexible showerhead enhances safety in that space as well. A bed rail not only offers security at night but also helps with transfer into bed. Proper lighting throughout the home ensures safe movement from room to room. Having a rehab specialist come to the home to point out overcrowded areas and places where rugs or other items present a potential hazard contributes to prevention of falling.

3. *Increase convenience.* Keep frequently used supplies such as tissues and transfer belts readily available in the car and home. Convert to adaptive eating utensils. Such cups, plates, and silverware are available for purchase at medical supply stores or online.

4. *Enhance communication.* Telephones with large numbers and rings with enhanced volume can be found at specialty stores or on specialized Internet sites. Setting a cell phone to family or emergency contact numbers can be helpful. Phones with limited options make use easier for individuals who experience difficulty with a multistep task.

5. *Support mental sharpness.* Find supportive academic material to help the individual maintain reading, writing, and computation skills. Bring in materials to make story problems more concrete. Work puzzles, discuss current events, and keep a journal together.

When the care receiver experiences a change in condition, a special educator/caregiver may find that the person they support needs to move to an assisted living community or skilled nursing facility. Like a home in need of adaptation, these environments also incite the instincts and induce the imaginations of special educators. The needs of the adults remain with the potential capacities and interests of these adults in mind, as special educators naturally detect ways to match these needs with specific accommodations.

Having been at endless IEP meetings, a special educator feels right at home during his or her care center counterpart, the care conference. Before attending, the teacher might choose to organize subject matter for discussion, categorizing it under the headings of speech therapy, physical therapy, health issues, psychological and spiritual supports, and social opportunities, as applicable. Just as multidisciplinary teams meet in a school, professionals gather in adult facilities in a similar fashion. Here the teacher makes an impact on the agenda, care plan, and, consequently, on the quality of life the care receiver has at the facility.

Special educators see potential wherever they are. They may, for example, upon noticing a natural area on the grounds of a facility, suggest a group "field trip" to look at plants and birds. They see such an outing as an opportunity to volunteer and to be with the family member they support.

Maybe in the past the person now at the care center went out into the community for shopping or for religious services. A special-needs trained caregiver might figure out a way to use city buses with lifts in order to maintain continuity in lifestyle. A special education teacher knows how to find a new path to the same outcome.

Just as a special education teacher developed expertise on teaching students with various IDEA-defined areas of disability, so also can a teacher become an expert on the medical condition of the person they support. This helps them understand the issues and see the path for assisting the person. Gathering such knowledge may even lead to the presentation of a training session for staff members.

SUMMARY

Incorporating adaptations and accommodations when at school comes from applying what is noted on a student's IEP and from the instincts and training of the teacher. The skills are used when working with students across environments.

The skills also come out quite naturally when the teacher moves into the role of parent or engages in various forms of community involvement.

When special educators travel, the ability to adapt comes to the fore. When they encounter various challenging personalities in public, they rise to the occasion. When caring for a vulnerable adult, they know how to access parallel models to those at school and find assistance in setting up a disability-accessible home to support the person. The adaptation skills of the special educator serve them and others in many ways at school, at home, and in the community.

REFERENCES

Donovan, M. (2009). *Email interview with author, Mary Z. McGrath,* January 15, 2009.

Fedje, L. (2009). *Email interview with author, Mary Z. McGrath,* January 16, 2009.

McGrath, M. (1995). *Teachers today: A guide to surviving creatively.* Thousand Oaks, California: Corwin Press.

Reano, C. (2009). *Email interview with author, Mary Z. McGrath,* January 27, 2009.

Chapter Ten

The Ability to Focus on the Individual Needs of Others through Ongoing Assessment

Brent had been a bird-watcher since he was a preschool child. He recalls enjoying the opportunity of going on such outings with his mom and her group. He came along because she preferred to keep him with her instead of dropping him at a sitter or day care center.

Even before that, so he is told, she carried him on her back in a baby-wearing sling when she went bird-watching. While he slept, nestled against her, she had both hands free in order to quickly bring her binoculars to her eyes when she saw movement in the bushes below, or trees above, as well as action in the skies.

As he grew older, he learned by observing the skills of her group. Certainly she told him to scan the skies and environment, looking for a change or the unusual. He was fascinated with how these avid birders could pick out a variation in the landscape, fix their scopes on this potential sighting, and determine that it was a bird.

They were able to visually hone in on the bird, who was attempting to camouflage itself due to its keen ability to spot subtleties. By looking at the field marks, the bird-watchers then made the distinction not only between species but subspecies as well. They liked to talk about the seasonal plumage differences, too. The very same bird could hide in winter snow and then at another time blend into summer woodlands.

Brent also looked back on his elementary education. He was forever stumped as to how his teachers could catch students who were not paying attention. When anyone passed a note, looked out the window, gave a friend an eye roll, or slipped a piece of candy from their desks into their mouths, the teachers saw it. These teachers seemed, as the old saying goes, "to have eyes in the back of their heads."

Thinking further on these two common settings of his childhood, Brent wondered if there was a connection. Upon entering the local state university, he felt pulled in two directions about what he would choose as a major. Should he go the science route and even become an ornithologist, or consider special education? He knew he was visually sharp and alert to what was going on around him. Perhaps, if he went into special education, he would be able to use his observation skills just like his teachers did. As far as his interest in birds—what a perfect hobby to balance out the challenges he would face as a special education teacher.

As his mind wandered between both past areas of experience, Brent thought of how often the bird-watching experts found various species through listening and identifying their particular songs. How would his sharp hearing help him as a special educator? Certainly he would have to listen to students with his heart. In addition, he would need to listen to nuances in speech patterns, application of phonetic sounds, use of grammar, as well as intention and meaning behind social conversations among students. He realized that tone of voice indicates intent and the feelings behind the message. A sharp ear picks up on such detail just as it differentiates birdcalls.

A skill that truly amazed Brent was how birders could instinctively find a bird. It was as if they could read the bird's behavior and plan of action. Even when a bird sat quietly attempting to hide, these avian enthusiasts seemed to follow their gut to get to the exact habitat to locate a particular bird they needed for their life lists. They were very focused and used their eyes, ears, and instincts to zero in on their individual target birds.

Going with his gut would be a perfect talent for work in special education. Brent would be able to read student behavior, figure out who stole an object from another's desk, and determine the best personality combinations for small-group work. Just as he had learned how to predict bird behaviors, Brent would also be able to apply his instincts to learn the ways and wiles of his students. With a sharp and innate ability to know others, he would be able to see the potential and talent of his students as well.

Brent, with his astute eyes, acute ears, and developed intuition decided to begin basic studies at the local university, keeping in mind the possibility of working as a special education teacher someday. When he told his mother, she was stunned. It was amazing to hear that having included Brent when following her passion for birds, she had laid the groundwork for his future career. She envisioned not only attending his graduation but also observing him in action as a teacher of children with special needs.

ASSESSING STUDENTS AS A
PROFESSIONAL SPECIAL EDUCATOR

Teachers working in the field of special education assess students in both a formal and informal way. In order to determine if a student qualifies for special services, the teacher serves as a member of the evaluation team and administers academic tests developed to indicate student proficiency in basic skills such as language arts and math and also uses instruments to determine their ability to function in various environments. Certainly an accomplished special educator knows how to administer a formal test as directed from manual specifications or in-service training.

In addition, the teacher also makes notes throughout the testing session of various academic as well as social features of the student's actual work, words, and actions. As a teacher listens to the student read various passages, the student may struggle with aspects of the reading process. For instance, the student may be able to read only the first part of a polysyllabic word. If so, the student will likely require instruction in syllabication. Maybe a student will guess, repeat, or skip certain words, telling the teacher about the mastery level of vocabulary, decoding, distractibility, or visual acuity.

Questions lead to more questions. Clues from the student can be topics of conversation for an assessment team. Maybe the student has been taught by a method incompatible with learning style. If so, the child may have done well in spite of instruction, and with a method that is a better match, the child will succeed.

When tested for comprehension skills, a student may falter in various ways. Observation notes help a teacher to evaluate and then later determine what strategy would best build skills. In the future the teacher may want to further support the student in sequencing story events or noting in more detail features of the story setting, for example. Performance with a short passage may appear to be only a snapshot of student progress, yet for a special educator trained to catch detail, student reading can be telltale on many levels.

When a student is writing a response, the teacher observes whether spelling is correct according to the dictionary or phonetic according to sound/symbol relationship. If the teacher finds phonetic spelling and can "read" the word, understanding what the student intended to say, the teacher makes note. Here the teacher learns if a student is a visual or more auditory learner. Upon making this observation, the teacher gets a clue from the student about how he or she should be taught to spell. Learning word families may be just the thing for one, whereas for another, memorization of words as they are presented will work just fine.

If a student reverses certain letters repeatedly, that tells the teacher that the student could have issues in terms of how the brain processes visual information and represents it through writing. This notation will remind the teacher to check with a school psychologist to see if other testing data indicates this. The special education teacher could then check in with the classroom teacher to see if writing samples verify the observation of reversals. If reversals appear to be a pattern, the special educator will know ways to help the student write these letters with more consistently correct formation by using strategies incorporating the kinesthetic and tactile modalities.

When a student is given the opportunity to compute basic math problems, they will likely show mastery of certain processes. With other sample problems, they may attempt and get to a certain point in a problem and be unable to continue. For instance, in long division, they may start strong and then stop. Perhaps they would need help in recalling steps for solving this kind of problem. Maybe a division error shows the student has yet to memorize a certain division fact. If a child cannot memorize facts, then they can be taught how to access this information. While doing math testing, a teacher noticing number reversals will respond the same as when discovering letter reversals.

When working with story problems, a student may have difficulty reading them and do well when the problem is read to him. It is up to the teacher to make such distinctions. When applying math skills in ordinary life, a student may not do as well. Maybe a student's comfort with rote learning, coupled with the inability to make life application with that information, would be indicative of student cognitive ability. This discovery may match the results found by the testing psychologist. Putting informational pieces together helps shape potential future service for the student.

In addition to visual and auditory data that teachers gather, their instincts and personal judgments could be another means of verification. One of the authors spent time recently with a former coworker. When discussing the assessment process, this former teacher noted that experienced special educators realize when they are testing a child with a disability. The reality is that some students need special modifications and alternative instruction as a matter of course. Their brains work as they work and respond as they respond. Thus it is up to trained teachers to note telling observations throughout the assessment process.

Required formal student observations bring a helpful dimension to the assessment process. When a sharp special educator watches behavior and records it via a required checklist or through narrative, they capture a segment in time. Yet such snapshots tell the team what the teacher typically sees, or they bring out alternative information from those who normally see other behaviors as well. Often when one of the authors went into a classroom to observe student behavior, the teacher expressed frustration that the child put on his or her best when the observer was there. This discrepancy, however, helped the teacher express priority concerns.

Even though a special educator does not see everything, they know, again through the use of prepared interview questions or informal exchange, how to gather and assemble information from those who spend extensive time with the student being assessed. They also know how to file in their minds information they have heard about students during casual conversation with building personnel. They learn what happens on the bus, in the cafeteria, and on the school grounds during social and sporting events. They know the value of watching, listening, and following their instincts in locating information on students, putting it together to see the full picture of student learning and behavior and then responding to student needs with instructional and behavioral plans.

One instinctively looks at students, their environment, and the exchange of both as they assess students on a moment-by-moment, day-to-day basis. With trained eyes and ears and instinct, the special educator scans the classroom, the gym, and the hallways, ever watchful of academic, social, and behavior successes or red flags. When a teacher notices a student accomplishment, she knows it is time to raise the bar of expectation. When a teacher notices a student struggling, he knows it is necessary to repeat instruction or determine a new strategy to address the same concept.

When special educators notice the start of an altercation between students, they know that it is time to intervene in order to prevent conflict. If conflict is well on its way, the teacher may have to bring in another adult in order to diffuse the situation.

A teacher may pick up on more subtle behavior cues when watching and listening to student social interaction. Accompanying intuition tells the teacher who is accepted, who is lonely, who is hurt or angry. Teachers watch their students engaging in social exchanges for signals that they are in need of support or ready to express aggression. Tears or tone of voice tell the teacher to consider context and predict the potential direction of the exchange. Observation leads to ways school personnel determine how to assist students in forming stronger interpersonal bonds.

By watching, listening, and intuiting, in combination or separately, special educators fix upon essential information to advance students academically, socially, and emotionally. They determine the means to remedy educational gaps, build social bridges, and prevent conflicts when students lose their grip on reason. Through awareness of students as they progress through the days and weeks of the school year, special education teachers build upon information from past formal and informal tests and observations in order to bring their students forward to further academic success, social competence, and emotional maturity.

ASSESSING IN THE ROLE OF CAREGIVER

Imagine Brent, now in his fifties, at the pinnacle of a successful career as a special education teacher. He has worked with students with various disabilities and seen them succeed in subjects that may have been daunting without his application of special methodologies. Beyond his abilities to use special strategies for learning and behavioral support for his students, Brent is now at the point in life where he is using his skills to support his mom. With macular degeneration, her vision problems are such that she can no longer enjoy going on bird-watching outings. In addition, she struggles with balance as the result of a minor stroke. Now in her eighties, she is no longer able to live independently.

Since Brent's dad died of cancer in his early fifties, Brent has supported his mom in various ways, such as doing home repairs and often including her with his family for meals and movies. However, now it seems that his mom's situation is such that his efforts are insufficient to help her manage on her own. Consequently, Brent has decided to search for an assisted living facility for her.

Since Sunwood Assisted Living Community is located right near his school, Brent has planned to check it out after work. Still in the mode of special educator, his visual and auditory assessment skills accompanied his instincts as he entered the building. This combination created the perfect lens to examine the facility. He mused as he entered that he has passed this place so many times going to and from work, yet he had never been inside.

Brent noticed a receptionist sitting at a desk and asked her if it was possible to tour the building. She was slightly abrupt with him but hurried to get a manager. After she left, Brent happened to notice a novel opened and turned upside down at the side of the desk.

Brent had to wait for twenty minutes for the manager. When she arrived, she shook his hand quickly and introduced herself as Mrs. Greenwood while offering him little eye contact. She began the tour, pointing out the carpeted parlor, people enjoying a card game, and new chandeliers. She commented that families come often to visit their relatives and even stay in a guest apartment on the premises. At this point Brent gave Sunwood mixed reviews. He was less concerned about the cosmetics and more concerned about the care. Those in charge had done little to connect with him. He wondered if they typically connect effectively with the residents.

As the tour progressed, Brent decided to look carefully at the appearance of the residence and residents, looking not only for clean rooms, bathrooms, and dining area but also for proper grooming of the residents. He was also interested in checking their affect to see if they seemed adjusted and supported at Sunwood. While he passed through the halls and common areas, he also listened in on interactions between staff and residents for cues as to how the staff treated and cared for them.

After a half-hour tour, Brent thanked Mrs. Greenwood and left for his walk around a nearby partially frozen lake. A brisk walk would offer him the time to sort out the pros and cons of Sunwood. Certainly the front area of this well-designed complex looked impressive. Fine furniture, top-of-the-line carpet, lovely paintings, and plenty of lighting would impress any visitor. However, as he walked the path, various other impressions came to the surface of his mind. He had noticed more than one wilted plant in common rooms, dirty floors in the dining and recreation areas, and many full wastebaskets in resident rooms as he passed by.

Faces of several individuals entered his mind. He remembered a man who looked like he had not had a shave for several days. A woman wearing hearing aids sat in front of a TV turned on high volume. She did not appear at all interested in the children's cartoon show blasting before her.

Brent recalled exchanges between residents and aides in which the residents were spoken to as if they were young children. Aides addressed them using terms such as "honeybunch," "grandpa," and "cutie." He thought his mom, a woman of dignity and confidence, would find this demeaning. Brent also happened to overhear two staff members speaking with one another while administering medication, talking around the residents as if they were invisible. Their focus was more on their weekend plans than on the task of the moment. This disturbed him because his mom, being a highly social person, needed opportunities for participation and conversation.

When Brent moved in and out of the areas and among the staff and residents of Sunwood, he felt uneasy. His instincts told him that his mom would not receive the quality and level of care that she now needed. Tomorrow he would call Mrs. Greenwood and thank her for her time but tell her he needed to look further.

The next day, Brent shared his observations with his team teacher, Jen Holloway. Jen thought for a moment and then told him about a care center in the next town. She had heard from her neighbor that people received good care there. Brent resolved to check it out the next day. He wondered if it was premature to "put his mom in a nursing home," but he decided to go see the place anyway.

On the following day, Brent headed out of town, looking at the puddles from melting snow now forming in the cornfields along the way. When he entered the care center, the director immediately left his desk and came up to introduce himself, wearing a pleasant smile and warm expression. He offered to take Brent through the facility and answer any of his questions. Brent did notice that the front area was nothing special to look at, but thought he would give the place a chance.

When they went through the halls, he saw people that appeared well-groomed sitting in wheelchairs or moving about with the assistance of a walker or hand railings on the walls. Staff members appeared intent on what they were doing at the moment, as they engaged the residents. However, when they could, staff members glanced at him and acknowledged his presence. Generally the people living there seemed calm and secure in their demeanor.

When Brent passed by one room, a man acted quite agitated because he could not find his photo of his daughter he believed to be in a particular drawer. Although busy, the aide, who addressed him by his first name, Frank, took time to help him search for the photo. Down the hallway an occupational therapist worked with a woman to properly position her in her wheelchair.

The tour included a community bingo session. Staff and local volunteers sat by those who needed assistance, placing the large, red markers on the boldly printed cards. Family members came and went, appearing at ease and seeming to have access to staff when they needed them. In fact, one adult son came up to the director and asked if they could talk. Though the director excused himself, Brent overheard parts of their conversation as he sat in a nearby common room and read the paper. The man was frustrated because his mom was not getting the dessert she enjoyed most, and the director promised he would look into it for the man.

Brent did not need time to decide what to do for his mother. Though he had not taken his "thinking time" walk, the down-to-earth atmosphere and respectful staff indicated to him all he needed to know. He asked for an application form and promised to return for a visit with his mother the following afternoon. Brent relied on his skills during both visits and capably decided where his mom would best be served and supported at this next stage of her life.

Using eyes, ears, and instinct, special education teachers automatically do the same when in the role of caregivers, not only supporting family or friends needing assistance but also responding to what they observe in order to lend immediate assistance and determine appropriate direction for family. The following are seven ways that special education teachers use their abilities when in the role of adult caregivers.

1. *Check upon arrival.* When teachers visit vulnerable adult family members or friends, whether at home or in a facility, they automatically survey the person from head to toe. They notice subtle and immediate changes in appearance, expression, and demeanor. If the person appears alert or confused, they notice and respond accordingly. They know if the individual is in an improved condition or whether he or she needs to ask questions of the staff.

2. *Keep a log.* Special educators document everything of importance. As when assessing a student, they keep notes in a way that helps them report their observations to facility or medical personnel. When at a care conference or medical appointment, they bring lists of priority topics for discussion, take notes, and prepare accordingly for the next meeting.

3. *Maintain confidence in what they know to be true.* Just as special educators respect the insights of parents, they respect their own as well. Subtle changes in manner or expression may go unnoticed by busy staff, yet one who knows and observes catches speech and communication changes. They spot a bruise or a balance glitch. They sense when the person has something to say but is hesitant to bring it up. They notice a change in grooming from when the person was more independent.

4. *Look below the surface.* Perhaps the vulnerable adult only appears different due to a minor scratch on the forehead. To determine the potential source, a special educator may watch how the person, when in a prone position, is turned to the side during a sponge bath. Perhaps the person was turned too quickly and bumped against the wall. When the teacher notices small sequential bruises on the arm of the adult resident, they may suspect that someone gripped him or her too tightly and left the imprint of their fingers on the person. They document this information and suggest that the staff move the person more gently in the future.

5. *Solve problems.* Special educators are not only trained to notice problems but are also trained to look for solutions. For example, if a person sits leaning in one direction, they think of ways to help bring the posture into correct position through the use of a pillow or wedge form. When the person's head falls forward, they find a small towel, roll it up, and place it under the chin so the person can look forward instead of watching the floor. When presented with any kind of problem, they will not walk away unless they have put effort into a solution.

6. *Apply concepts to new environments.* Just as school teams develop IEPs for students, so do care center teams plan for a resident with a personal care plan. Once a special educator sees this system, they operate with the same understanding as they had for student IEPs. It is a matter of taking an educational paradigm and transferring it to a new environment and new

people. Special educators evaluate the needs of their care receiver in order to determine level of service, whether it is home care, assisted living, or a care center where skilled nursing is provided.

7. *Consider possibilities.* Having operated with the concept of least restrictive alternative, special educators work to enable their care receiver to maintain as normal a life as possible. For example, if the person attended church regularly, the special educator will find adapted transportation so the person can continue doing so. The special education teacher believes in routine. When a family member moves into a facility, the teacher works to include routine radio and TV shows that were formerly part of the person's life. If the person enjoys the outdoors, the special educator will team with care center staff to plan an outing. Special education teachers are comfortable dreaming big because they have worked to bring their students to their full academic, social, and emotional potential. Keeping the world of the care receiver comfortable and familiar, yet broad and stimulating, remains a constant and meaningful challenge for special-education trained caregivers.

After both formal and informal assessment comes action; and in taking action, a special educator makes a difference across environments. Whether in a school or a care center, a special education teacher relies upon visual, auditory, and intuitive information to act for the benefit of students, family, and friends.

SUMMARY

Special education teachers use their visual, auditory, and intuitive abilities to assess students in the school environment by using formal instruments and informal strategies. This is a continuous part of the job. When given the opportunity, they transfer the same skills to consistently support family members or friends needing care and assistance, whether in their own homes, assisted living communities, or in a care facility with skilled nursing support.

Chapter Eleven

Problem Solving

Lisa has been working as a special education resource teacher for a district for about fifteen years and has made herself well-known for her pleasant demeanor, wisdom, and problem-solving capacity. She has enjoyed her reputation as being an amicable and caring person. The district administrators are very pleased with her. They feel she is an asset for them because she handles challenges and issues effectively. The principal of her school relies on Lisa's expertise and values her opinion.

She has a unique ability to stay calm in difficult situations. She knows how to detach and still be able to work with an emotional situation. Therefore, she finds herself pretty much at ease even when she is dealing with difficult parents or belligerent students. Parents find her easy to talk to, approachable, and open-minded. She uses social skills effectively: effective listening, respectful communication, negotiation, and conflict resolution are a few of her strengths.

Lisa is fully committed to children with special needs and always looks beyond students' disabilities to enhance their potential. When she receives an evaluation of Lindsay, one of her third graders, identified as having learning disabilities in math and writing, she engages in developing a meaningful individualized program (IEP) with her team. She finds that she and the IEP team are able to develop goals in math with no problems. They all agree that Lindsay needs to work on two-digit multiplication with regrouping. Mr. Newth, the general education teacher, is fine with how Lindsay will be handling her math in his classroom. He will be explaining how to analyze the problem and then how to solve it, and Lindsay will receive additional instruction in the resource setting.

However, Lisa notices issues with developing appropriate goals for writing. The team decides that Lindsay should receive instruction in writing in the general education setting. Lisa knows that Mr. Newth is unable to provide one-on-one attention to students with disabilities in his class. He has thirty students in his classroom receiving instruction in the six steps of the writing process. He uses a three-point rubric to evaluate different types of writing products. The rubric does not necessarily measure the small increments and changes in writing.

Lisa knows that Lindsay should use the six-step writing process and should work on these writing components on a daily basis. At the same time, she is fully aware that Mr. Newth will not be able to find sufficient time to evaluate Lindsay's written work. This lack of continuous feedback may not be helpful to Lindsay. Lisa knows that Mr. Newth needs to prioritize the goals based on skills that Lindsay needs to strengthen. She also knows that his classroom is not structured to create opportunities for frequent feedback.

As Lisa draws the attention of the team to Lindsay's needs, the team struggles with establishing objectives for each writing skill that Lindsay needs to learn. Understanding that Mr. Newth needs assistance with how to teach based on Lindsay's experience and learning capacity, Lisa offers her assistance in working with Mr. Newth, which he gladly accepts. She fully understands that Mr. Newth is not making excuses for not teaching or evaluating Lindsay's work; it is truly difficult to address the needs of thirty students at one given time.

A problem can be an opportunity knocking, a chance to get out of the rut of routine, and an occasion for a different way of handling a problem and making a situation better. Whether problems are routine or atypical, whether common or rare, in all cases Lisa has developed a positive attitude toward them. She is willing to access relevant information, seek advice if needed, look at a variety of options while planning for future actions, and assist in carrying out solutions. She examines all sides of the current state of the problem, tries to remember what the goal is, and then becomes a part of the solution. She uses her problem-solving skills within the classroom and outside the classroom in her everyday life.

Special education teachers like Lisa develop a flexible repertoire of problem-solving strategies by working with various children and youth with disabilities, such as cognitive disabilities, autism, emotional disabilities, learning disabilities, and other health impairments. As they work with these children, they become responsive to students' individual characteristics and understand how to support their learning by modifying the curriculum to meet their needs. Right from the beginning of the planning process, they engage in problem solving for each child they serve, which goes through the steps of prioritizing goals and objectives; making instructional and curricular adjustments as they need; and constantly refining decisions about curriculum and instruction. They know that no matter how much they try to anticipate learning, they may have surprises with which to deal.

WORKING WITH A VARIETY OF PROFESSIONALS

As soon as a special educator makes the professional decision to become a special educator, he or she knows they will have to collaborate with a variety of professionals, which include general educators, paraprofessionals, school counselors, speech pathologists, occupational therapists, social workers, etc. In teacher preparation programs, usually, special educators receive instruction and training in how to work in teams so they can engage in collaborative problem solving. Since services for children with special needs are rendered by various professionals, related service providers, and community agencies, they learn to work with various professionals, paraprofessionals, and families.

Special educators use these collaborative problem-solving skills in their everyday lives. As they try to resolve conflict within the family, they problem solve. When they work with service providers for themselves, they must engage in collaboration.

As they collaborate with professionals and agencies, they identify and address specific problems, communicate about various options, engage in dialogue with colleagues to understand the extent and depth of issues, and strive for better options for students who need them. They view issues and problems as opportunities to reflect and refine their own practice.

IEP Meetings

In the IEP meetings, special education teachers demonstrate problem solving by being analytical, creative, and practical about student concerns. They look at the term *problem* as an issue, concern, or a need for change, rather than an obstruction or hindrance. They conceptualize problems as changes that need to occur in the learning environment that might impact the child's ability to be successful in that academic setting.

Before they make any decision, they engage in data-based decision making and collect information from a variety of sources to make an educated decision about the extent of the problem, special services that the child needs, and the best way to provide these services. They show willingness to revisit their decisions and reflect upon them with their colleagues to make changes as appropriate.

Making Instructional and Curricular Decisions

Special education teachers develop a unique capacity to use a variety of instructional techniques to promote student learning. For example, Jason, a first grader, has a tough time asking for help. He keeps quiet and pretty much stays undetected until Mike, the classroom teacher, goes closer to him and finds out that he is struggling.

While teaching social skills to Jason, who has difficulty asking for help, Mike, the special educator, teaches him the skill of recognizing when and how to ask for help. Mike prompts Jason to ask for help when the moment arises, then reinforces him for this assisted version of the desired behavior. When Jason independently asks for help, Mike uses a stronger reinforcement for this independent behavior. After that, he asks Jason to self-monitor the number of times he engages in this skill.

Depending on the type of disability, special educators use certain teaching methods that include individualized instruction, cooperative problem solving, and small-group work. Special educators become flexible with these structures and show fluidity in transitioning from one structure to another. When students need special accommodations to take a test, they know which accommodations are appropriate ones, such as reading questions orally, lengthening the time allowed to take the test, providing extra physical space, and increasing the font size. As they decide on which of these accommodations are reasonable, they are constantly examining which of these would serve as a better option for a specific student.

UNDERSTANDING THE COMPLEXITY OF LEARNING

Special educators understand the effects that disabilities may have on a child's learning and behavior in school and throughout his or her life. Instead of viewing special needs as deficits or problems, they look at them as opportunities for teaching differently. They try to make learning accessible to their students as much as possible.

They also look into the contextual factors that influence pupil learning. Learning as a complex process is influenced by beliefs, traditions, and values across and within cultures. For example, how meaningful is it for a student from an Asian background to learn the skill of maintaining eye contact? What is the relevance for this skill in the American context? What will the student be missing if he or she does not learn this skill? How would learning this specific skill assist in the overall social functioning of this student? So the special educator is constantly engaging in a cost-benefit analysis of each skill.

Moreover, the special educator actively seeks resources and guidance from families to understand how primary language, culture, and background may have an impact on the individual's academic and social abilities, attitudes, values, interests, and career options. In other words, they look at the associative factors that help in understanding the problems better and developing solutions for them.

This sociocultural understanding provides the foundation upon which special educators individualize instruction to provide meaningful experiences to students with special needs. They use cultural knowledge, prior experiences, behavior, and learning styles of students with special needs who come from diverse linguistic and cultural backgrounds to try to make learning more appropriate and effective for them by acknowledging their cultural heritage. They reflect upon how their own identity interacts with people with linguistic and cultural differences. As we all work and live in a very diverse society, special educators use these skills every day.

Aside from the fact that special educators emphasize individualized educational programming as a key component, they also prepare their students for successful community living. They are aware of the benefits of connecting the general and special education curricula to meet the needs of students with disabilities. While individualizing instruction, they emphasize direct instruction of skills, strategy training, self-monitoring, and programming for generalization of learning. To augment student learning, they carefully increase access to the general education content by selecting and adapting materials, instruction, and curricula. In all these activities of teaching, they are constantly engaging in the process of problem solving, determining why the student is not learning, what the strengths of this student are, what they need to do to teach him or her differently, and how they need to make learning engaging for this student.

SHARED DECISION MAKING

Traditionally, special educators taught their students in resource or self-contained classrooms. Although working in these settings gave them independence and protection, they also became isolated from the rest of the school community. Now they are faced with bigger challenges of shared decision making, where they are expected to work in teams and combine their professional knowledge, perspectives, and skills. They are expected to collaborate with general education teachers, which has opened up new roles for special educators that range anywhere from providing assistance to the general educators to co-teaching with them.

Often they share goals, decisions, instruction, responsibility for students, assessment of student learning, problem solving, and classroom management with the general education teacher. In this shared decision-making process, sometimes they need to adopt a new consultative role and work with the student with special needs in various environments, which requires them to constantly engage in the problem-solving process to come up with better solutions. They may feel like the "rules" that exist for learning for many students do not apply to their particular situation or that they are facing a new problem for which they need to develop their own solution.

Understanding Learning Environments and Learning Differences

Suzie moved from New York to work in an urban elementary school located in a southwestern state. The school three years ago was characterized by low test scores, poor attendance, and generally unmotivated students and was considered a failing school. Not only did it have a high turnover rate of teachers but also the teachers who stayed appeared to be burnt out and ineffective. It appeared teachers cared more about protecting their own jobs than helping students.

Suzie made a deliberate choice to go and work in this school because she knew she could make a difference in the lives of students and families. In three years, Suzie began to problem solve by affiliating herself with like-minded people in the surrounding area. They created a group of four teachers who met frequently and shared some social and professional experiences together. They were willing to try innovative approaches with their students—they were willing to educate with methods that seemed unconventional. To address the issue of reading problems of some students, they considered using comics in their classroom—they knew these students liked reading them and were not engaged by other reading materials. These teachers decided to put away their negative preconceived notions and give comics a try. As a result, in three years, they were able to show improvement in reading scores in their classrooms.

Without getting flustered or frustrated, special educators show unique ability to respond to learning differences and willingness to explore options and meaningful resources for students with special needs.

Steps of Problem Solving

Special educators try to understand "what is the problem?," "why?," how often does it occur?," and "what is maintaining this problem?" For example, Susan, a second-grade student, throws a fit in the third period of reading when asked to read aloud. Using a functional behavioral assessment procedure, Lori, the special educator, finds out the function of the fit and focuses on some contextual factors that trigger her behavior. Lori knows that once she has an understanding of why Susan gets upset every time she has to read in third period, she has a better chance of solving this problem and she can come up with better interventions. So she begins to look at some contextual factors, the reading material, where she sits in the classroom, and Lori's technique of teaching reading. She figures out that in one-on-one reading, Susan is fine. It is only when Lori asks Susan to read aloud that she throws a fit.

Special educators also figure out why it is important to study these problems and the obstacles that the problem presents. When asked to read aloud, Susan not only stops reading, her behavior also interferes with other students' learning. In Susan's case, Lori tries to analyze the meaningfulness of this behavior. In doing this analysis of the problem and its relevance, the special educator also attempts to figure out which of the aspects of the problem are under his or her control. Without jumping to conclusions, they ensure that they have all of the information and that they have analyzed it carefully and looked at it from various viewpoints. As they go through this process, they try to be as objective as possible, refrain from being judgmental, and use critical-thinking skills.

After analyzing the problem, they engage in the decision-making process. If they need to engage in collaborative decision making, they communicate with various professionals, administrators, parents, and paraprofessionals and they mediate when conflicts occur and determine various options or solutions. They analyze and evaluate options, evaluate how and which of these options seem reasonable, and examine the pros and cons of these options. After evaluation of these options, the special educator is ready to act on the well-thought-out solution. The problem-solving process seems to take many steps, but with constant use, it becomes automatic for special educators.

SUMMARY

This chapter highlights the problem-solving role of special educators. In this role, they show an ability to identify a problem, to generate solutions, and to evaluate solutions to identify better options for the existing problem. They analyze what aspects of this problem they have control over, what can be changed or altered, and what needs to be identified as an unalterable situation. Without jumping to conclusions, they engage in a systematic process of collecting information from relevant sources and then determine options that may serve as solutions. Special educators apply this important skill throughout life—they avoid jumping to conclusions without all of the information that is needed, they assess all sides of a story, and they develop potential solutions.

Chapter Twelve

Collaboration

Norma Anderson, a special educator at Freeman Elementary School in a midwestern state, teaches fifth- and sixth-grade resource students. She really knows how to effectively collaborate with general educators, paraprofessionals, and parents. Recently, she attended a seminar on collaborative science teaching and thought that the information that she had received would be beneficial for everyone in her school, particularly those involved in teaching science. She invited the principal and general educators in her school and a few parent volunteers to an informal lunch to share what she had learned.

Parents at the school have been voicing their growing frustration at the school's decision of fitting science into students' hectic day. Norma was unsure about how much of this information would be positively received by her colleagues and parents. But she was going to try.

Norma held the meeting after school in the media room and showed some charts and figures on a bulletin board to explain how to use the concept of science as an approach to problem solving for fifth graders and how this approach can help students improve their thinking skills. She gave a few examples of how she would go about this for the first semester. She facilitated the discussion and generated some ideas from the group. Everyone agreed that it was worth a try.

Norma offered to set up an orientation for the parents. She asked for volunteers, and three parent helpers and the science teacher agreed to help her by co-teaching with her. She identified three units, electricity, magnets, and gravity, to be addressed in the first semester and set a biweekly schedule for science instruction in six fifth-grade classes.

Parent helpers assisted in setting up and breaking down materials for each lesson taught. Norma and her team debriefed after every session and reflected upon what was successful and what changes could be implemented next time.

At the end of the semester, they came together and discussed whether or not they should use the problem-solving approach to teaching science the following semester.

During these reflections, they reviewed the strengths they observed that included: 1) students with disabilities were included in these science lessons; 2) parent volunteers not only felt enthusiastic about science but they also offered their time to assist in the lab; 3) later in the semester, after hearing of this success, the sixth-grade teachers asked Norma to include them in this endeavor; and 4) the district science specialist came out to observe their lab.

After much discussion, they agreed that they should adopt this method of teaching science. There were academic benefits for all students, including those with disabilities. Students with disabilities started asking questions about the machine, gravity, electricity, forces, and magnetism. They also checked out books on these topics just for fun!

In this example, Norma used the following steps to collaborate.

1. Attend a professional development activity (workshop, conference, training, etc.);
2. Offer to staff and parents an opportunity to share what she learned;
3. Schedule a meeting to introduce the content;
4. Decide how the new approach will be implemented (teams, etc.);
5. Decide how the implementation will be evaluated;
6. Schedule follow-up meetings;
7. Implement;
8. Evaluate and decide if the implementation was successful or what could be improved.

Following Norma's example, Marcy, the reading specialist for the school, returned from a conference on instructional strategies and shared her new learning with her colleagues. There were five reading and six math teachers from all of the other grades who wanted to learn from her. First, she thought she could not collaborate with such a large number of teachers at one given time. However, after giving it some thought, she decided to organize and divide them into two separate teams, reading and math.

The two teams met on a weekly basis, and every third week they met as a full team. She asked each subteam, math or reading, to focus on how they intended to define the outcomes and common assessments. She also encouraged them to brainstorm strategies for teaching reading or math skills and concepts to the students. The teams developed plans where they could observe their peers using a specific strategy in their classrooms.

Marcy explained that observing was more than seeing. In fact, they needed to observe multiple aspects of learning and multiple ways that addressed learning difficulties. Over time, each team member became confident in their colleagues' ability. The teachers reflected on how their students were doing, how they were improving in various areas and showing their strengths, and where their teaching seemed ineffective. Then they became comfortable in sharing their ideas with the other team members.

After each team had an opportunity to present its recommendations to the full team, they shared the differences between instructional strategies and fun activities. In the beginning Marcy noticed that veteran teachers in both teams were used to doing things a certain way and had little incentive to change their practice. Marcy did not even talk to them about changing. However, they noticed that the school data demonstrated that their students were not achieving as much as other students. As a result, by the end of the year, they became motivated to explore why and started to gain interest in the collaborative practices.

Fostering relationships with colleagues, parents, paraprofessionals, and other constituents is a difficult task. The reasons may range from a difference of opinion to the lack of time to connect with each other. In the beginning of the year, Suzie, a middle school teacher, really had a tough time collaborating with Mary, a resource teacher. She was more of an "information hoarder" and did not want to share knowledge, resources, or materials. People like Suzie see knowledge as a source of power and do not want to share it. When Suzie realized that she could benefit from Mary too because Mary also has a wealth of information and lots of resources to share, she became friendlier toward her.

Mary had a variety of programs and resources for teaching social problem solving to middle school students. She was very successful in teaching conflict resolution to these students. The assistant principal sent students who received disciplinary actions to Mary to learn social problem solving and conflict resolution. Later in the semester, Suzie started collaborating with Mary to assist a couple of students in her seventh grade classroom who were likely to benefit from social problem solving.

Special educators understand that they work in a school, which is a part of a larger community. When they think they are in need of professional assistance, advice, or specialized knowledge to meet the needs of their students, they 1) contact various agencies and professionals; 2) collect various resources; 3) use strategies that seem to influence the thinking of special educators who have traditionally been working in isolated environments such as positive peer pressure and data-based discussions and decision making; and 4) share new ideas and experiences that cause them to act in new ways.

The collaborative environment, where teams of educators work together on the vision, mission, and goals for their school, agree on effective teaching methods, and make curricular decisions, creates positive *peer pressure* for every educator involved. This positive pressure enables special educators to stay professionally involved at every level of decision making and stay abreast with new research and ideas.

Most teachers want their students to reach their learning potential and, for that, they commit themselves to continual professional learning. They learn strategies that will enable their students to perform better. Professional learning occurs when there is a planned effort within a school where each educator has an opportunity to interact, ask questions, learn new ideas, and examine the effectiveness of new learning and to reflect upon how to make changes and adjustments.

Professional learning communities emphasize data-based decision making, and all the members of this community act as a team. Data-based decision making occurs when educators collect meaningful data, examine data, and make decisions based upon data. Special educators work as a part of a larger community to support student learning and productivity. In recent years, the nature of the job for special education teachers has changed significantly. As a team member, they work with general education teachers, parents, administrators, and other school personnel to provide an appropriate education that meets the needs of their students.

Despite the push for inclusive practices, special educators continue to acquire the specialized knowledge and skills training relevant to the needs of students with disabilities, and they continue to apply their expertise to assist other high-risk students in more collaborative educational environments. Their role goes beyond school support specialists and includes multiple responsibilities. They identify the educational needs of students with disabilities and gather information from multiple sources to better program for educational success. They know how to connect assessment with instruction, differentiate instruction, and make appropriate accommodations and modifications for students with disabilities.

In some settings, they serve as transition specialists and work with other agencies such as vocational rehabilitation centers and technology centers to facilitate transition of students to postsecondary settings, like community colleges, technical, and vocational schools. To facilitate the academic and/or adaptive skill development of students with diverse learning and behavioral needs across a variety of educational environments, they work with various professionals.

As instructional specialists, they collaborate with general educators across a variety of subject areas using large- and small-group teaching methods and apply a variety of instructional methods, i.e., direct instruction, cooperative group techniques, activity-based approaches, and other appropriate techniques. To meet the needs of students who are identified with serious behavioral or mental health issues, they work with counselors, social workers, mental health professionals, and other health agencies.

So what is collaboration? Collaboration is a process of joint planning, decision making, and problem solving that occurs in a variety of formats: between two individuals, small groups, two or more agencies, and formal or informal groups. Participants in this process share goals, processes, decisions, and outcomes. We see that special educators collaborate at three levels: individual, school, and community.

Individual level refers to when a special educator decides on his or her own to collaborate with other professionals. At the *school level*, the school system decides that all educators within that system will collaborate to produce better outcomes for their students, and the special educator participates in the joint decision making and partners with others. At the *community level*, the whole community of stakeholders, including parent advocacy groups, institutions of higher education, the state department of education, school districts, and detention and secure care systems work together to ensure that students receive the best possible education. The special educator participates in the community of decision makers and advocates for children with special needs.

INDIVIDUAL LEVEL

At the individual level, special educators decide what will work better for their student and seek out information and assistance as needed. Students with special needs differ in the ways that they best learn and express themselves. Thus, to increase access to an appropriate education for their students, special educators teach in various formats. They co-teach with content area teachers, i.e., science teachers or math teachers, engage in small-group instruction, or provide one-on-one instruction in a resource room setting, etc. For students who have serious learning challenges, they use functional curriculum that enables their students to have community living skills and independence. In addition, they facilitate the learning of students who have communication problems by integrating assistive technology.

For example, Daniel and Patty are science teachers in a middle school, and they collaborate with each other on science teaching for seventh and eighth grade classrooms. Lisa, the learning disabilities resource teacher, uses some lessons of science for her seventh grade resource students. She decides to meet with Daniel and Patty to see how she can develop and integrate conceptual explanations that her students can understand; she develops additional learning activities and games and creates opportunities for practice for her three seventh grade students (Jason, Susan, and Mili) that meet with her three times a week.

She creates a unit on gravity using multimedia that is followed by interactive lessons, printable worksheets, and assessments to assure student's mastery. She meets with her colleagues, Daniel and Patty, to see how they are planning for instruction for the seventh graders. She then looks at the IEPs of these three students and decides to break large chunks of instruction into small parts. She integrates hands-on instruction with traditional methods and switches to a different instructional modality, specifically for Jason, because he has a problem with attention.

With Susan, a seventh grader, she goes to the lab period and uses laboratory time for one-on-one instruction. She finds that Susan seems to be successful when she works one-on-one with her. Mili, another seventh grader, is high functioning and shows high interest level inherent in science subject matter. Lisa encourages Mili to attend science with her regular education peers in Daniel's classroom. Mili benefits if she sits right next to Daniel, the science teacher, where he can keep an eye on her and ask her to avoid sitting closer to the high-traffic areas.

To summarize, there are various ways for special educators to collaborate at an individual level. Another example is co-teaching, where two or more teachers can plan, teach, and assess the same students. Co-teaching is a way of teaching where a general educator and a special educator (or other special services professional) share responsibility for planning, delivering, and evaluating instruction for a group of students. They are trained to foster and maintain professional collaborative relationships to support student learning and well-being.

In other areas of life, special educators collaborate with a friend or friends to plan a support system for a mutual friend who is undergoing a series of treatments for a serious illness. They may collaborate at the individual level by taking a graduate class together or planning a trip together. Collaboration skills serve the special educator well throughout life.

SCHOOL LEVEL

At the school level, collaboration is one of the key factors that enhances the capacity of the building community and leads to reform and school improvement. With collaboration, special educators can greatly increase their expectations and do more for students with disabilities to better meet standards of learning performance. At this level, collaboration does not happen automatically, it needs to be systematically programmed.

In the routine of a school, there has to be a designated time for the special educator to meet with the general educator and other professionals. They need to have a meeting place where they can collaborate with the team when they develop the IEP goals for children with special needs or collaborate with other professionals when they develop an instructional policy and when they serve on a committee responsible for curriculum development and professional development.

For effective collaboration at the school level, special educators like Lisa 1) decide why they need to collaborate and who they need to collaborate with; 2) clarify goals and outcomes with their collaborating partners; 3) develop a common understanding about assessments; 4) develop a process about collaboration, time, location, responsibilities, etc.; and 5) examine results of their collaborative efforts to create new understandings.

At the school level, the culture of collaboration is promoted by inviting community groups to participate in or cosponsor school events. Special educators help schools in seeking specialized expertise of community organizations for providing professional development opportunities for staff. In addition, schools show their collaboration by offering space for community events and assist in keeping the school community and families informed of new ideas in education.

Collaborating schools tend to have satisfied teachers who enjoy their jobs and are likely to stay for a long time. In schools where teachers want to keep things the way they are and view change as uncomfortable, even scary, they have a tough time collaborating with others. They may communicate with each other, but they share ambiguity, apprehension, and no excitement about new learning.

COMMUNITY LEVEL

At the community level, special educators participate with various stakeholders, such as parent advocacy groups, professional organizations, state departments, and institutions of higher education. In these partnerships, they share their vision for student learning and teaching students with disabilities with others.

For example, there is a group called Access Education (a fictitious name). Teachers from all school districts in Mona County in a southwestern state; the state department of education and certification unit; parent advocacy groups; professors from liberal arts, education, criminal justice, special education, psychology, and speech and hearing sciences; academic professionals and practitioners from social work, psychology, and counseling work together on how to best serve children.

Teachers bring in ideas and examples of lesson plans and share with the members of this professional organization. All members demonstrate common commitment to collaboration, and they all feel responsible for decisions they make. If students drop out, they do not blame parents or general educators for not keeping them in classrooms or legislative or regulatory bodies for not having strict enough laws or policies. They all share the responsibility for their students.

Norma happens to be a part of this group. She truly enjoys how this group has created a community that cares. She really likes it when she receives acknowledgment of her birthday or small gifts or tokens of appreciation from time to time, compliments, or statements that reflect respect. The group organizes two annual events where they invite everyone involved with their families. Norma never misses the two events—she really likes this opportunity to engage in positive interactions between school faculty and leaders and to develop her leadership and power sharing.

When someone tells Norma collaboration is too difficult, she models how she collaborates with various professionals. When someone complains, saying that collaboration slows things down, she shows them how collaborative efforts have helped create innovative solutions for her and her students. She keeps herself abreast of the mandates under which schools must operate and participate in such discussions. She serves as a facilitator for the fall welcome that is organized to meet and greet the honors college education majors from a nearby university.

These skills of collaboration are incorporated into the special educator's everyday life. The special educator has to work together with her family members to resolve issues related to schooling, who is going to do what around the house, where the holidays will be spent, and how the family is going to cut expenses in this difficult economic situation.

When the special educator's parent is in an assisted living facility or in the hospital, the special educator must be able to collaborate with multiple agencies, physicians, nurses, and other caregivers and come up with agreed-upon solutions that are satisfactory to the parent who may have very particular ideas about what he or she wants to happen.

When the special educator is trying to make a major purchase, he or she has to seek information from a number of sources and come up with a decision that is the most satisfactory product-wise and economic-wise.

SUMMARY

Special educators are not only expected to collaborate with general educators, paraprofessionals, and parents, they know that they are a key driver for many decisions that are beneficial for students with special needs. With emphasis on inclusive practices, there has been a significant change in their roles (that has traditionally been individual). Teachers now work together on so many more aspects of the position that in the past had been done by one individual. They share the IEP goals, instructional decisions, problem-solving approaches, and classroom management processes in order to meet their students' needs and ensure that they know about community resources to promote successful transition to postsecondary opportunities.

Chapter Thirteen

Advocacy and Empowerment

Mr. Earnest has been a special education teacher at the high school level for thirty-five years and is approaching his retirement. He has spent endless hours reflecting on his decision about whether to retire—should he or shouldn't he leave his classroom? He has been a tireless advocate for his students in his cross-categorical classroom and he worries about what will happen to his students when he is no longer there. When coaches tried to refuse to let his students try out for the ball teams, Mr. Earnest was there to remind them that the law states that special education students have the right to try out for sports. When teachers refused to make accommodations for his students, he would work with those teachers to increase their awareness of the law that requires accommodations for students with disabilities. He would also assist the teachers in making accommodations. He learned quickly the importance of collaboration.

Perhaps what Mr. Earnest is most proud of is how he taught his students to stand up for themselves. Many of his students have graduated and moved on to the workplace or to postsecondary options. A number of them have graduated from college and have invited him to their college graduations. One student, Max, attributed his college graduation to Mr. Earnest. He wrote to Mr. Earnest: "I would have never made it through college if you hadn't taught me about my disability and what I needed to do to advocate for myself. I knew I had to tell my college instructors that I have a learning disability and I need accommodations. You taught me to use my disability as an opportunity to teach my instructors how to meet my needs."

Mr. Earnest contributed a great deal in his community as well. Together with his students he made a presentation to his school board about what his class was doing. He invited the school principal and superintendent to his classroom. He offered to speak at service organizations like the Kiwanis and Rotary. He spoke about the needs and accomplishments of his students. He was a member of the Lions Club and participated in their many service projects.

Because of Mr. Earnest's involvement, he understood the importance of volunteerism and taught that to his students through a variety of service projects that he incorporated into his classroom. His students participated in food drives and volunteered at a day care center and a nursing home. His students learned that others needed them, and they could make valuable contributions.

Mr. Earnest has been very active in his professional special education organization; he has served as state president of the organization and is now serving on national committees. While he will miss his students, there are many things he now wants to do in his organization and he is finding it difficult to have the time to do everything.

In the end, he decides that he will retire and will work with his national and state organization to assure that the rights of his students are protected. He also wants to work with special education teachers and parents throughout the country to stand up together for the rights of students with disabilities.

ADVOCACY

Good special educators advocate for their students with disabilities to make sure that the students get the services to which they are entitled. Many people think of advocacy as a negative term and equate it with being a troublemaker within the schools. However, being an advocate involves positive action to represent the needs of the student and the conditions under which the student will learn in the most appropriate way.

True advocates are those individuals who we admire greatly—we can all think of advocates throughout history—individuals like Rosa Parks and Martin Luther King, Jr. These individuals stood up for their beliefs. They had passion for a right and just cause. Their passion and advocacy came at great personal sacrifice—but they continued because they knew they were fighting for the right thing. True advocates are defenders of a just cause—they defend services for the students with whom they work.

Special educators enter the field because they have a passion for working with students with disabilities. Good special educators have also learned that they must advocate for their own needs in order to better serve the students. The special educator advocates for adequate materials and work space and better working conditions in order to meet his needs and the needs of the students. If the special educator finds himself assigned to a classroom that is very small, the special educator knows how to advocate to secure a better working space. The special educator knows what is needed to meet the needs of his or her students, and those student needs are the cause for which the teacher advocates.

Advocacy focuses on actions oriented to meet the needs of individuals. Throughout life we must advocate. We advocate for our own children to make sure that their needs are met. We may advocate for our spouse when he or she is being verbally attacked by others. Many of us are now advocating for the needs of our parents or other elderly individuals. There are issues raised today about elder abuse, and we must work to assure that our own parents are not abused in assisted living facilities or in nursing homes. We accompany our parents or our spouse or our children to the doctor's office and there must advocate that the individual's needs are being met.

There are people from education who serve as ombudsmen for elderly teachers who are in nursing homes who have no one else to advocate for them. If individuals who cannot advocate for themselves have no one to represent their needs, those individuals can be taken advantage of and abused or neglected. The advocacy skills we acquire being special educators prepare us for our everyday life of representing the interests of those who may not be able to represent themselves.

Knowledge Is Power

The best advocates are those individuals who know the laws and regulations that govern services for students having been identified with special needs. Good special educators don't take the word of someone else about what the laws and regulations state—they know the information themselves or know how and where to access the information. Good special educators must have the special education laws and regulations at both the federal and the state level at their fingertips. If they don't have a hard copy of the laws, such as IDEA or the state laws, they know exactly where to find the information.

Special educators will encounter colleagues who pretend to know the law and who will try to intimidate them with that knowledge. Recently, one of the authors received an email from a special education teacher saying that her building principal had told her some information about recent changes in state special education class size limits. Her special education supervisor told her very different information from what the regulations actually said. She needed to know which person was explaining the special education class size limits accurately. While the author gave her the information, she also told her where she could access the information on the Internet so she would have firsthand correct knowledge.

There are a number of ways the special educator gains this information—she keeps copies of the special education laws and regulations at her fingertips, and she knows how to access the information online. Because laws and regulations change, it is critical that the special educator keeps current with any changes that have occurred.

As a result, the special educator will need to know where to go to get the most current information. The special educator uses the Internet, belongs to his/her professional organization(s) in order to stay current with the latest information, attends workshops to make sure he is current in information, and also becomes active in his/her state organization in order to know what is happening. Because special education is litigious, the special educator must stay current with Supreme Court cases that impact special education and any legislation that is pending that will impact students with disabilities.

To make sure that special educators keep current with what is happening, they have learned the importance of documentation. It is important to keep logs of behavior and then review those logs to search for patterns. This documentation is an important life skill. An excellent special educator who is a good friend of one of the authors has been a longtime advocate for children with disabilities, and she applied her skills to her husband, who had surgery for a brain tumor. He couldn't advocate for himself, so she learned that she needed to take charge of his medical care and advocate for what he needed. Each time a nurse or doctor came into her husband's hospital room, she wrote down when they were there, what they said, and what they did. To advocate, she had to have excellent records, which she did have. She had knowledge on her side. She has since shared her strategies with others. She taught one of the authors the importance of documenting every action that takes place in the hospital setting.

Awareness

Awareness connotes alertness and sensitivity to the issues faced in the field. In order to effectively advocate, the special educator must be alert to the key issues facing the field of special education—what are the financial problems that are being faced at the federal, state, and local level that could impact special education services and who are the key players who are impacting the field? Perhaps there is a new local superintendent in the school. The special educator makes himself aware of that individual's viewpoints about children with disabilities.

The special educator is never complacent. Special educators are very aware that there may be good times for services for children with disabilities and there may be very bad times, and those times can change rapidly. The authors are always reminded of the fragility of services for students with disabilities. At the federal level in 1975, the law passed that provided a free, appropriate public education for all students. Programs and services were developed. It was an exciting time for special education. In the early 1980s, there was a change in administration and there were major efforts to remove services to students with disabilities. The authors learned quickly that the special educator must always be aware of changes in the political wind.

The special educator attends conferences, workshops, and school board meetings to make sure she is aware of what is going on. Good special educators are "lurkers." They lurk around meetings and conferences and hearings, listening closely to what other people are saying and at the same time voicing their opinions on what needs to happen.

Special educators have learned that if they don't expand their horizons by being lifelong learners, political forces can jeopardize the very field that special educators have devoted their lives to improve. They know that they must focus their efforts both within and outside the classroom in order to be the best advocates.

Collaboration for Advocacy

Special educators often find themselves being in the minority in a school building. They may be the only special education teacher who works in a school building full time—other special education teachers may be there part time or be in a situation where the speech therapist or school psychologist visits the school but is not there all the time. If there is more than one special education teacher, the special educators are still in the minority within their school building—the majority of the personnel there are general education teachers. Even if a special educator is in a specialized school where all the teachers are special educators, the special educator needs to work with the general education teachers in order to integrate her students into regular classes.

Because special educators are often the minority, special educators have learned the importance of collaborating with others. They know that it is critical that they work with the general education teachers. They do that both informally and formally. If they are in states where there are teacher's unions, they belong to those, making sure that the needs of the special educator are heard. They offer to work on committees or to chair committees. They may run for office—recognizing that they have the opportunity to make an impact on decisions made.

Informally they network with other educators within special and general education. They belong to other organizations whose members consist of a wide range of educational backgrounds. They listen to what others are saying and educate others on their viewpoint.

Special educators must work within their professional organizations to achieve their goals. It is sad that many young educators are no longer choosing to belong to their professional special education organization because they see no need to do so. However, belonging and being active in such an organization is a key to a special educator's success. The special education teacher on his/her own may not be able to advocate for regulatory or legislative changes that would benefit her students. However, if he or she is an active member of the organization, she can provide relevant input about key issues and work with her organization to see that needed regulatory or legislative changes are made. As an example, one of the authors was very concerned about some possible changes in special education teacher certification. She was active in her professional organizations and worked with them to accomplish the desired goal. Professional organizations fight for the rights of their members to the extent that their members provide input and become involved actively.

Belonging and being active in one's professional organization provides the tools that the special educator needs to better advocate. Networking with others provides fresh ideas for the special educator. Networking also allows individuals to connect with other special educators who may be facing the same challenges.

Collaborating with parents and other agencies is also critical in the special education advocate's role. There will be times that the special education teacher finds himself or herself in a difficult position. The special educator knows that the child needs more speech/language services than the child is getting. The special educator may speak up and request more services, but the parent has a critical role in the provision of services. The special educator can let the parent know that if the parent is concerned, the parent can request another IEP meeting to discuss additional services.

The special educator can and should make parents aware of their rights to services. The special educator can do that both directly and indirectly. Special educators are to give parents a copy of their rights and explain those rights to the parent. Even though there are administrators who believe that parents should not be given that information, it is mandated in IDEA. Special educators can also provide information to parents about parent training centers in the area, support groups for parents of children with disabilities, and organizations that advocate for the rights of parents, such as the Learning Disabilities Association of America. They can provide parents with notices about parent training workshops in the area or statewide conferences.

The special educator works closely with the building administrator to advocate. The channels of communication are kept open so that the administrator is aware of what the special educator needs for his or her students. There is definitely a chain of command within the school district, and special educators learn that in order to advocate effectively, they must communicate with the building administrator and other supervisory staff. There is no need to go to higher authorities within the school district if the administrator or supervisor can provide for the needs of the students and the teacher. If the special educator has gone first to the building administrator and still is unable to get what is needed, it is critical that the special educator documents the discussion(s) that have been held with the administrator and the action or lack of action that took place. The special educator can then go to other administrative staff with documentation and with the knowledge that he or she went to the first-line authority before doing so.

Standing Up for What Is Right

Special educators work to make sure that their students receive the services that they need—to do that they must stand up for what is right. Doing that is often very difficult because the pressure within a school system can be very strong to go along with the tide and to not make waves. It is often tempting to take the path of least resistance and to succumb to the pressure, but the good special educator knows that he or she must not do so—the special educator must be strong because the actions he or she takes will either positively or negatively impact a child's life.

During her career, one of the authors has had the opportunity to participate in thousands of IEPs. IEPs are the determining factor in the types of services a child will receive. That determination is so important because it can either be a deciding positive factor or a deciding negative factor for the child's entire school career. These authors have witnessed individuals who have done their homework—they know the child well before they ever go into the IEP, they have either been part of the assessment team or have reviewed the assessment report, and they clearly delineate their professional judgment about what the student needs. They know that their input is valuable, and their input must be grounded in evidence.

On the other hand, some individuals view the IEP as just another meeting—they come in unprepared by not having reviewed the records of the student, and they really aren't interested in what the child needs. They may only be concerned that their time is being taken for this discussion. Those individuals are not ones that the field of education needs because they are doing harm to children as a result of their lack of interest in what the child needs. Oftentimes, IEPs get bogged down with decisions that are based on what is available in the district rather than on what the child needs. Teachers are afraid to speak up at the IEP because they fear that the school principal or the special education supervisor will reprimand them. They forget that the IEP team decision is based on consensus, and they have a right and a duty to voice their opinion about what the child needs. They not only have that right—they have an obligation to speak up for what the child needs.

A special education teacher participated in an IEP for a student for whom she had provided services for three years, and it was now time for the student to move to the middle school. She had found that a particular accommodation—a small laptop computer—assisted the student tremendously in taking notes in his general education classroom. She shared this information at the IEP meeting. The next day she received a written reprimand from her special education supervisor who said that her comment about the need for that particular accommodation was inappropriate because she had not cleared it with the supervisor before discussing it in the IEP. The special education teacher knew her rights and went to her local union representative. She also provided the union representative information about what the law stated in terms of discussion of accommodations. The special education teacher and the union representative were successful in getting the written reprimand removed from her file.

This special education teacher could have easily been intimidated by the special education supervisor, but she was not. She knew that what she had done was legally correct and important to the best interest of the student, and she refused to back down.

Special education teachers will often find themselves in a precarious position when they stand up for the right thing to do. Yet they know they must work to do what is right and needed for the student. They have discovered whom to work with in order to get services for the student, and they have also learned how to get these services for the student.

Standing up for what is right, not being intimidated, and having a strong knowledge base are traits that serve special education teachers well through life.

EMPOWERMENT

Special educators feel empowered themselves to make a difference in the lives of their students, and they also model that empowerment with their students. They not only model it but also they teach their students how to be self-empowered. In an earlier chapter, we discussed the importance of teaching students self-management skills, and empowerment is one of those skills. Believing that they can and will make a difference is that sense of empowerment.

At the Learning Disabilities Association of America Conference, 2009, keynote speaker Cal Crow said it well: "Believing that you are capable of performing a task is as important as actually having the capability to perform it"(Crow, February 27, 2009).

Self-Empowerment

Most special educators have come into the field because they believe they can make a difference in the lives of children with special needs. They are committed to helping others who may not always be able to help themselves. They see the profession of special education as their calling and are eager to fulfill their purpose in life—to serve and assist others with special needs. To advocate effectively, they must be self-empowered. They believe in themselves and know that they can impact their students' lives positively. As part of that sense of empowerment, they create relationships with their students and believe that they are the key to the student's success and will work to the best of their ability to assure the student's success.

Understanding and Accepting One's Own Needs

A critical component of empowerment is knowledge of what one's needs are and accepting them and being able to voice those needs to others in order to get appropriate services. The special educator has learned to accept his own strengths and weaknesses in order to do a more effective job. As an example, if the special educator knows that she has difficulty remembering information that is given to her orally, she knows that she must write the information down. She knows that she needs to be honest with others and tell them that she has difficulty remembering information—by doing so they may be more willing to write down what they need. How many times have we heard someone say: "Can you write me a note to help me remember that?" Such a statement tells the other person honestly that you have difficulty remembering something told to you, and it also meets your needs. To reach the students with whom the special educator works, the special educator must know himself. The special educator understands his own strengths and weaknesses and also knows and recognizes when he or she makes a mistake. When the teacher does make a mistake, she is not afraid to let her students know that she has done so.

Teaching Students to Be Empowered

In a previous chapter, we discussed the importance of teaching students self-management strategies. The adults who work with the child are not always going to be around to advocate for the student—the student may find himself alone when he enters the work world or the postsecondary world. He must learn to advocate for himself and stand up for what he or she needs within those settings. The student must feel empowered to make the difference in his own life.

The special educator must teach the student from an early age about his strengths and his weaknesses. The more the student understands his specific disability, the more the student can begin to understand his own needs and how to get those needs met.

Many people frown about providing a label for a student. They don't believe that any labeling should occur. For any of us who are medically diagnosed, we know that we find comfort in understanding why we are not feeling good or why we are having specific pains. If we have heart disease, we want to know that so we can then seek the appropriate treatment for ourselves. Such is the case with providing a label for a student. A student may very well feel relieved when he is told that he has a learning disability because he can understand that he is intelligent but has a specific disability for which he needs to learn both remediation and compensation techniques.

One of the major issues facing our students with disabilities is their desire to not disclose their disability and try to make it on their own. One of the first things the special educator must do is to teach the student as much as possible about his or her disability and teach the child that there is nothing to be ashamed of by letting people know about the disability. In order for the student to receive services, the student must let people know what he or she needs. Part of that self-awareness is learning about one's own strengths and weaknesses and how to build on strengths and seek assistance for weaknesses.

The belief in oneself and knowing that an individual can make a positive difference in this world serves the special educator well throughout life. The special educator sees something that needs to be done and feels empowered to be able to accomplish that task.

SUMMARY

Special educators envision themselves as advocates defending the rights of a cause in which they believe—assuring that students with disabilities receive the appropriate services to meet their individual needs. They are defenders and protectors of their students. They are empowered to fight for a just cause. Their passion for this cause is the impetus for them to make a difference for each of the children they serve. Their empowerment and advocacy skills remain with them throughout their life—defending and protecting those in need.

REFERENCE

Crow, C. (2009). Identity, self-efficacy, and resiliency: Touching the heart and soul. Keynote Speech at the General Session of the Learning Disabilities Association of America Conference, February 27, 2009.

Chapter Fourteen

Family Support

As the pressures on families and teachers increase, working together provides the greatest opportunity for students' success. Let's visit one special education classroom where this successful partnership has lead to improved academic and social learning. Inside a self-contained special education classroom in one urban high school, Paula, a special educator, is committed to the education of her students who have mild to moderate intellectual disabilities. Through her commitment to students and her own professional learning, she has developed valuable ideas and skills of how to involve students' parents from the community in providing outstanding educational experiences to her students.

You can immediately feel her enthusiasm for teaching as you enter her classroom, which is filled with positive energy and personal engagement. Walking down the hallway, her principal, Mr. Nelson, looks into the class and smiles before continuing on his morning walk-throughs. Having solid support for special education from the principal really helps Paula build and maintain beneficial relationships with parents.

Paula's principal identifies the importance of the function of special education and treats all educators as professionals. He commends and supports Paula's idea to organize a special night twice a year for the parents of children with disabilities to share ideas and spend time together as a support network. On this special night for parents, she serves pizza or burgers and encourages parents to get to know each other and share resources. After they meet, many offer babysitting support to each other when they have IEP meetings, library visits, or other school-related events. The principal supports the event by attending and being available for parents at that time.

Mr. Nelson understands that students with disabilities need a variety of services and are better served if the school collaborates with families. His school provides a full continuum of special education placement options, ranging from inclusive classrooms to highly specialized, self-contained classrooms. He makes an effort to understand how special education works and encourages parents to participate in the decision-making process for placements of their children with special needs.

Twelve students are in Paula's class, and all receive special education services as students with mild to moderate intellectual disabilities. There are also two paraprofessionals in the classroom that support academic instruction and provide behavioral supports. Jason, a fifteen-year-old who has cerebral palsy resulting in spastic diplegia, needs physical supports to move around in his wheelchair. Paula has considered his mobility needs in arranging the classroom so that he has full access to classroom spaces and materials. A paraprofessional is assigned to work with him one-on-one and help him in his physical movement from one place to another.

Paula ensures that Jason engages in academic and vocational learning. She provides multiple opportunities for Jason to use functional vocabulary. Whenever an opportunity arises for him to speak, she prompts him to say a few words by asking short-answer questions and respectfully allows time as he attempts to produce the words. She has taught the other students to follow her modeling and not speak on his behalf. Jason also uses his communication board to communicate with his teacher, paraprofessional, and peers.

In addition, Jason has a communication partner to interact with him in an authentic way. Three tenth-grade buddies come to his classroom twice a week to model how to produce relevant words, and they practice new vocabulary with him. He seems motivated by the interaction with his same-age peers, and Paula has measured improvements in his speech.

Jason enjoys one-on-one time with the paraprofessional on the computer. He has designed menus to use with his communication board for various local restaurants so he may order independently, and he has created bookmarks, charts, flyers, and even artwork displayed in local museums. He is well-versed in computer technologies and applications. He creates PowerPoint presentations for his peers, edits them carefully, and puts in graphics and music for them.

Students in his class help Jason by taking turns in assisting his movement around the classroom, in the cafeteria, or on the playground. While he is riding his electronic wheelchair, he seems to have great control over his spasms.

Jason's mother, Sara, approaches the tasks of daily living activities (eating, grooming, and working) and education very seriously and expects that Jason will make gains in his independent living skills as he completes his high school education.

Jason's brother, Scott, attends the same school and is in ninth grade. Sara reports that he is doing well in the honors' program, particularly in math and science.

Sara is perceived to be the family advocate for the school system and shares a reputation for being antagonistic, determined, and sometimes threatening. She goes to all the Individualized Education Program (IEP) meetings and is a member of a parent advocacy group that provides the most current information on resources for children with mild intellectual disabilities. She keeps up with the new school policies and laws and seeks out any new information that may have ties to Jason's success.

One of Sara's concerns for Jason is that he develops his independence. She wants Jason to participate in a vocational program entitled Transition to Independence during the summer. This course is generally opened for twelfth graders who are identified as having physical, sensory, and mental disabilities. Unfortunately, as a tenth grader Jason does not qualify for this course this year.

When Sara approaches the principal, he resists this idea and tells her that space is not available for Jason in the program this summer. But, he adds, that he will make an exception and will ensure that Jason gets a space next year. Sara, however, thinks that the principal must make an exception for her son, even though he is only in tenth grade this year. She is anxious about Jason and wants to ensure his future does not get compromised because of his disabilities.

Paula knows that Sara is unhappy with the principal's response. Paula understands that Sara really wants to support Jason—emotionally, socially, physically, and financially. As a mother, Sara knows about Jason's mental and physical challenges, but she does not want to stop his growth and wants him to have the same advantages as any other student getting this opportunity. While she maintains the normal routines of her family life, she spends a lot of time trying to learn about Jason's educational needs.

Paula understands that Sara is looking for an opportunity that would enhance the potential for her son's independent living. Paula keeps Sara informed of the daily school routines and announcements and makes sure that she has a voice for Jason in the decision-making process. Paula shares new information, Internet resources, and Internet discussion groups as well as selected journal articles that relate to vocational training for individuals with intellectual and physical disabilities.

Paula has a great reputation with the parents of students in her class. She always shows respect for families and their values and cultural beliefs and practices. She makes an extra effort to reach out to them. She considers them experts on their child. Sara and Paula have established a relationship that has benefited Jason. Demands from Jason's classroom and school add to Sara's stress, but Paula hopes her open communication alleviates some of the stress and knows that deep down all Sara wants is the best education possible for her son.

So what does Paula do about the summer course? She decides to go to the principal and ask if he would allow her to videotape the sessions and have Jason work with the taped materials. The paraprofessional will facilitate the learning. The principal supports the idea, but he wants to check with the instructor of the independent-living skills course before committing to the parent. Mr. Landers, the instructor of the course, states that he is fine with videotaping the sessions. When Paula tells Sara about her idea, she is thrilled that she has a partner at school to advocate for her son and that he will have an opportunity to access this important experience.

This chapter provides information for creating opportunities for family participation in special education classes and other school settings and makes the case that family support predicts children's academic achievement, social development, and emotional well-being as they progress through their school career.

Teachers of children with special needs, who are like Paula, make continuous efforts to learn about and from children and their families, structure opportunities for interaction with them, and develop a shared sense of purpose and common goals.

PARENTS: A CRITICAL RESOURCE

Special educators encourage parent participation at every step of the special education process and view them as a critical resource. They become supportive of parents and families and involve them in all major decisions related to their child's education.

Parent involvement must begin prior to the initial referral of a student for special education services. Special educators start working with general educators in teams and begin to involve parents in the education process from day one because they know that according to special education law, parents have a right to participate in the education process of their child. Thus, special educators collaborate with general educators to try early interventions and prereferral strategies that may assist the student.

Special educators help general educators in providing accommodations and supports for students before they are referred for special education services. For example, Susan, a third grade resource teacher, works with students who are at risk for reading problems. But she continually works with Amanda, the second grade classroom teacher, and assists her in providing reading instruction to a couple of students who are at risk for reading disabilities. This practice has prevented a few students from getting referred to a learning disabilities resource classroom in third grade. The skills that special educators have gained assist them in working collaboratively in the world outside the school. The special educator problem solves with others and always recognizes the important role that the family plays in everyone's life.

DEALING WITH DIFFICULT PARENTS

Sometimes special educators must deal with demanding parents who constantly disagree with the district's special education program and the school's policies and insist that their decisions are followed. Sometimes parents are uncertain about how to resolve conflicts; they do not understand the process of developing the Individualized Education Program (IEP) and fail to participate in a team-based process and show communication difficulties with the school district administrators. As a result, they get frustrated when school staff and faculty appear to ignore their requests.

Special educators, like Paula, try to understand the parents' concerns and show respect for the family and make a sincere effort to use parents' choices and preferences in establishing IEP goals and expectations. They attempt to build rapport with the parents by listening to them before sharing their own ideas about student goals or progress information. They use effective communication skills and recognize issues that may emerge ahead of time.

They use simple open phrases, such as, "I am glad to see you," "how can I help you?," or "what is on the agenda for today?," "do you have any suggestions?," and "what is your view?" to open opportunities for communication.

Paula places independent living skills as a top priority for Jason, followed by consumer/work skills, social skills, and character-building skills. She agrees with Sara, Jason's mom, in that all students need to be taught the skills for enhancing their independence and employability, including those who have physical or other disabilities. That is why parents like Sara have developed a great working relationship with her.

WHY INVOLVE PARENTS?

Increased involvement of parents and families is one of the most important ways of improving a child's education. Parent involvement not only influences the students' attitude, interest, and participation but also it adds to the relevance of the educational experience. When the student feels a part of the school community, he or she shows willingness, interest, and participation in various curricular and cocurricular activities. In the broader context of schools, when parents of students with disabilities are enabled to become effective partners in the student's education and are encouraged to participate in the decision-making process, the education process becomes meaningful for the student.

SUPPORTING FAMILY INVOLVEMENT IN SCHOOL

Special educators should engage in various activities to facilitate parent involvement in their classrooms and school. They should take the time to understand the families, their strengths and needs. By understanding family characteristics and needs, they can encourage parent participation in various ways.

Orientation

A special educator is fully aware that a crisis is not the best way to meet a child's family for the first time. Paula organizes an orientation in the beginning of the year and invites all her parents. She brings forward some positive anecdotes from her fellow teachers that show how many of the children, despite their challenges, have accomplished the goal of independence.

She encourages them to share their contact information with each other, so they can also feel like they belong to a community of parents who have similar concerns, issues, and situations. In this orientation, she talks about various local sources and services parents can access. If she gets an opportunity, she invites a local musical group or a pianist to play for a pro bono performance, and everyone seems to enjoy the evening.

Understand Family Needs

Special educators understand that some families participate by engaging in every aspect of the child's education while others need to know in general how their child is responding to a specific intervention, such as anger management, a behavioral intervention plan, or an individualized token system. Some families like weekly progress reports, others are satisfied with a monthly communication of overall progress. And some others don't want the school to send this information home. They say "I take care of home—you take care of school." Special educators know how to reach out to parents who have diverse needs for communication.

Some parents show their involvement in various ways: attending parent–teacher conferences; assisting in developing materials; serving as a parent helper; supporting school talent shows, cultural programs, and events; supporting social events, car washes, and field trips; and volunteering in art masterpiece programs. They are eager to participate in any activity they possibly can. Others have to be called in for a reason, and sometimes they may view these calls as threatening. Special educators make sure that they are pleasant in their communication to reduce unnecessary anxiety in parents. Special educators do not wait for children to fall behind or fail, but they are proactive and they begin to address the issues early on by notifying them of resources they can use with their children and seeking assistance from parents on how they can all work together to meet the needs of the child.

Show Interest in the Students' Well-being

Like Sara, many parents feel that their priorities for their child are not fully taken into account by schools. Particularly in the IEP meetings, parents often feel that teachers talk down to them, do not give them the opportunity to express their feelings and knowledge about their child, or use educational jargon they do not understand. Not only are special educators sensitive to parents' feelings but they also expect that parents will be engaged in the education of their child. They view parent involvement as a critical factor in a child's success in school. They also develop skills and competencies for effectively engaging them in various activities at school.

Make School a Welcoming Place

If the school is a welcoming place for families, they tend to get more involved with their children's education. As parents enter the office, they should feel they are welcomed in the school by every staff member and faculty. Special educators decorate their classrooms with materials and pictures that are likely to appeal to parents. They set up a family center run by parent helpers, whereby they create opportunities to meet, talk, and provide information or help with concerns they may have. Parents and teachers exchange ideas and create a context for new learning for themselves and for parents.

Encourage Participation in Social Events

Many special educators, in collaboration with their staff development specialists, participate in parent fun nights, talent shows, empowerment workshops, adult education classes, and parent training sessions. For example, Paula always asks her parents to join her on a tour of the neighborhood or she calls two or three parent helpers to assist her in planning a neighborhood tour, and she takes the children from her classroom out to a nearby bank and to McDonald's. Parents serve as chaperones and go with students on the neighborhood tour, and they supervise children and assist them in learning how to exchange dollars into coins from the bank and then buy an ice cream cone from McDonald's.

Exchange Positive Communication

Paula has established a regular system for sharing good news. Almost every week, she sends notes home and writes something very positive about children in her class. She always tries to show parents how much she values their child and sees his or her potential to succeed. She asks them to come after school when they are done with their jobs; sometimes she orders pizza and creates a nice, welcoming environment in her classroom. Specifically, she avoids negative discussions during her first visit with them. Throughout life, special educators have learned the importance of creating a welcoming environment for individuals.

Accommodate Work Schedules

Oftentimes families are criticized for not attending an IEP meeting or not responding to a report card. Special educators keep in mind the constraints of time and pressures of work that parents have. Meetings should be held before or after school to accommodate parents' work schedules. Many special educators stay open to meetings in the afternoons, evenings, or on the weekends to increase the possibility of having parents' presence in the meeting. They contact the parents to make sure that their preference of time is considered prior to organizing an IEP meeting.

Respect and Dignity

Many parents blame themselves for having a child with a disability; they feel embarrassed when their child is identified with special needs and assume responsibility for their child's disability. Instead of viewing parents as difficult, resistant, and the "source of the problem," special educators find them receptive and try to communicate with them. They take the time to talk to parents, asking them how they are doing. They inquire about their concerns and what might be on their minds and invite them to share their feelings. Any opportunity they get, they help parents in reducing their apprehensions and doubts and assure that they are a critical resource in the process of their child's education.

Parents Know Their Children

Special educators should rely on information from parents about their child with disabilities. Parents have a wealth of information about what their child likes, dislikes, and what seems to work with them and what serves as a trigger. Special educators use parents' views, ideas, and information and develop a level of trust with them. With a sincere effort to incorporate parents' views, they are able to provide a better learning environment for children with special needs. Special educators have learned empathy and work to see others' points of views and needs.

SPECIAL EDUCATORS LISTEN BEFORE THEY JUDGE

Often parents of children with disabilities develop acceptance about negative information about their child. They hear terms like their child is not grasping a concept, not reading, not paying attention, not understanding, is disruptive, belligerent, off task, or defiant. Many parents may already feel responsible for their child's disabilities, and after hearing such negative descriptions for a period of time, they begin to avoid school activities and communication. They start believing that they are never going to hear anything positive about their child, so there is no benefit in attending meetings. In such situations, special educators make an extra effort to separate parent's guilt from what the child needs—they show them the strengths of their child and help parents understand how they can assist in providing a better education to their own child. The ability to listen, rather than to quickly judge, is a life skill that serves special educators well. With their colleagues and friends, they know the importance of understanding what issues they are facing, and they listen well rather than making a harsh judgment about a situation.

SPECIAL EDUCATORS ARE CULTURALLY COMPETENT

Special educators know differences in social and academic behaviors that result from exposure to various experiences in life. They understand that all children may not display the same response to the same prompt or direction. Children from diverse backgrounds bring unique opportunities for learning and teaching. Just because Marcy does not ask questions in class does not mean that the teacher should not offer extra help. Marcy happens to be quiet and needs help in math. The special education teacher identifies students like Marcy who need attention and offers them help.

During cooperative structures of learning, special educators find students participate at different levels. Some take over the task, others submit. Some have a difficult time in cooperating with others because they like to do independent work. Some of these differences in behavior may relate to specific family values, past experiences, backgrounds, and cultures. While some cultures promote group work, others give importance to independent thinking. Depending on student needs, special educators seek appropriate training in culturally sensitive approaches to working with families.

REFLECTIVE PRACTICE

Special educators engage in extensive reflection to continuously refine their practice. From time to time, they step back and evaluate their own learning. They seek input from families they serve as they continue to grow in their profession. They look at their own stressors and take the time to step back and evaluate and adjust according to their own personal situations and professional goals. They examine their own lives and ensure that they provide themselves enough time for leisure and relaxation.

SUMMARY

Special educators encourage family involvement in a variety of ways, ranging from having positive communication and exchanges supporting the child's education to participating in a fund-raiser or serving as a classroom helper to advocating for children with disabilities. When families and special educators work together, they create a better climate for learning, leading to positive outcomes for students with special needs.

Conclusion

Marie loves her position as a special education teacher of students with varying disabilities but had been discouraged at the end of the school year. She didn't feel like she had accomplished everything she wanted to get done that year. She was worried that some of her students would lose ground academically over the summer. On the last day of school for the year, she received a letter from one of the parents of a student in her class. The letter read:

Dear Mrs. Caldwell:

I can't begin to tell you what a difference you have made for my son, Jordan. Until Jordan was in your classroom he hated school and would cry each morning that he didn't feel good and didn't want to go to school. For the last five years, our life at home has been in turmoil because Jordan hated school and kept falling further and further behind. Then Jordan came to your class—he loved your class and every morning woke up excited to go to school. He now likes to read and even does his math without any fights. You have made a big difference in Jordan's life and our entire family's life. I am delighted that Jordan will be with you again next year.

Sincerely,
Jordan's mom, Susan

Marie read the letter over and over again. She rethought the original discouragement that she faced. She reflected on the many talents that she had brought to her position. She sat at her desk and thought that this is all worth it. What better reward than to make such an unforgettable impact in the life of a student. One child at a time—she makes a difference through the many positive dispositions that she possesses and that permeate her life in and out of the classroom.

Special educators are a unique group of individuals who bring many positive attributes to their positions. Because of their complex role, they are adept at meeting the multiple challenges they face each day in their profession.

This book outlines those attributes and celebrates the talents of the many Maries who are out there every day bringing hope to students with special needs.

Frank Wood commented in his foreword that many people fail to understand the realities of the classroom and the many challenges it presents. The special educator rises to those challenges with great finesse and expertise. The talents that special educators apply every day become a part of their life routine and make them the successful individuals that they are.

When preparing to write this book, some of the individuals who reviewed it said they would like to use the dispositions that are discussed throughout this book as a guidepost to interview potential candidates for special education positions. They want to make sure they employ individuals who exhibit these characteristics. Individuals teaching at the university level found that this book would be helpful in teacher training. They can use these dispositions as a guidepost in their preparation of future special educators.

As a result, we have prepared the checklist below to guide individuals who are recruiting special educators and as a review of the dispositions that are discussed throughout this book. This was not designed as an exhaustive list but is designed to address the major attributes that the special educator should possess and exhibit in order to effectively work in the special education profession.

CHECKLIST FOR DISPOSITIONS OF SPECIAL EDUCATORS

- Tolerance for individual differences and freedom from prejudice
- Ability to actively listen and be empathetic
- Ability to establish a positive relationship with students while maintaining appropriate boundaries
- Ability to frequently recognize positive actions
- Understanding that respectful discipline is a teaching opportunity
- Ability to create and implement individualized educational plans
- Ability to see progress in small steps
- Ability to adapt
- Ability to focus on the individual needs of others through ongoing assessment
- Ability to problem solve
- Ability to collaborate

- Advocating positively for others' needs and recognizing their empowerment
- Ability to gain support and respect from the family

Each chapter in this book has spotlighted a different talent or personality gift that is exhibited both at school and in the family or community at large. Those of us who are special educators are who we are, and we work to conduct ourselves consistently across environments.

Our purpose in writing this book was to bring that awareness to fuller consciousness so we all continue to grow in these aspects of our professional and personal selves. It is important for the special educator to continue to grow as an individual. To assist our readers in their growth, we have provided a review of the chapters with questions for you, the reader, to carry forward to reinforce your awareness of who you are in all arenas.

The first chapter reviewed the myths that are often heard when individuals hear that you are a special education teacher. As you hear these myths, ask yourself these questions:

1. Are you modeling the real traits and strengths that you possess?
2. Are you educating others about your roles and responsibilities?
3. When you hear one of the myths, are you taking some time with the individual who voiced the statement to educate them about your role and why your work is critical?

Chapter 2 presented the importance of tolerance exhibited in the actions of the special educator. Tolerance helps you in approaching appropriate decisions for the student, maintaining personal connections, and establishing professional networks. It allows you to be approachable, flexible, and encourages you to gather information from various perspectives on an issue. As a professional, you need to ask the following questions:

1. Are you tolerant of differences and views that are not compatible with yours?
2. Do you reflect on your own prejudices and biases? What do you do when a student shares a belief that is against your belief system?
3. How do you engage in a process of gathering information to approach an unbiased decision?

Chapter 3 focused on the importance of empathy and active listening. Special educators take the time to listen and to decipher the message behind the words. You separate the words from the person. You view a situation with a particular student from that student's point of view rather than imposing your own values. As you move forward in the profession, consider these questions:

1. How do you practice active listening with your own family and friends?
2. When confronted by an angry individual, rather than becoming defensive, do you stop and attempt to view the situation that evoked the anger from that individual's point of view?
3. Are you working in all areas of life to separate the words said by an individual from the person, refraining from quick judgments about the person because of what they have said?

Chapter 4 addressed the student/teacher relationship and expanded the development of these exchanges into other aspects of life. As a special educator you work at being present and respectful to students. You make certain to reinforce and discourage behaviors as appropriate. (On the same day as this was written, one of the authors called a service company to request that the young man who had done work for her return to complete the job correctly. She pointed out what he had done well and showed him what needed to be finished. In addition, she built a relationship by showing him her travel maps on the walls and other items in the home. She thanked him for his efforts. He left with a smile since she gave him some chocolate as well.) Also, in these relationships you use appropriate boundaries and extend care and interest as you assess student need.

But it does not stop there. Consider the following questions as you go forward:

1. How are you present and respectful in everyday encounters, such as relating to the teller at a drive-in bank, the person next to you in the grocery line, your own children, family members, and friends?
2. How do you praise behavior that is constructive and discourage any behaviors in individuals that bog down a group or discourage others?
3. When you encounter individuals in social settings, how do you determine what you can do to support the person who shares a personal challenge while still maintaining appropriate boundaries?

Chapter 5 stressed the importance of recognition of the positive actions of others—recognizing both accomplishment but also the effort of others. It stressed the importance of setting children and others up for success. As you move forward, frequently ask yourself these questions:

1. Do I work to assure the success of others so that they can be recognized for their success?

2. Do I frequently monitor my own behavior to make sure that I am recognizing others' accomplishments?
3. Do I give credit to my students and others for their efforts as well as their accomplishments?

Chapter 6 focused on discipline challenges and the importance of addressing those challenges as an opportunity to teach. Rather than focusing on punishment when a child behaves inappropriately in a certain situation, we should provide logical consequences and teach the child the appropriate behavior. In the future, reflect on these questions:

1. Since I am a role model, do I set the example for appropriate behavior and accept consequences when I have behaved inappropriately?
2. Do I teach the appropriate behavior rather than waiting for an inappropriate behavior to occur?
3. Am I firm, fair, and consistent in my work?

Chapter 7 addressed the IEP writing process. Drafting such a document entails more than meeting with the team charged with putting together the particular IEP. Skills on the part of the special educator can make this IEP effective and impact a child's life, long term. Thus the preliminary testing and observation on the part of the teacher lays firm groundwork for a successful, accurate, and comprehensive individualized plan for a student. Before your next meeting and as you involve yourself in the lives of others, consider the following questions:

1. How well do you observe your students in order to directly address academic, social, and emotional needs in the IEP?
2. How do your observation skills apply in your personal life?
3. Since listening at the IEP meeting is a key skill, consider how that makes or breaks the team's success. Where else in your life do you apply your highly developed listening skills?

Chapter 8 revolves around one foundational principle in teaching special education—breaking tasks down into incremental steps. This concept makes learning concepts doable for students who have to take things one step at a time. Elsewhere in our lives we work better at a task when we break it down as well. With this principle in mind, ask yourself the following:

1. Bring to mind a particular student and mentally review a task that you are working on with that student. Can you imagine teaching this task as a whole and also in steps? Consider the outcome of each approach.

2. Look at your own life in terms of ways you assist in family, social, and community settings. Do you find yourself breaking tasks down, even unconsciously and automatically?
3. How do you benefit yourself and serve others by using an incremental approach?

Chapter 9 highlights the ability of a special educator to not only design and apply adaptations and accommodations for students but also the teacher's ability to move with flexibility among settings. A student group with particular difficulty adapting to situations are those on the autism spectrum. Ironically, when a teacher creates pathways for these students, he or she must be exceptionally flexible. Use the following focus questions to find your own skills at adapting:

1. What aspect of your professional work requires you to be the most adaptable?
2. What features of your home, school, or community involvement bring out this skill in you?
3. How might your flexibility and adaptability come to the forefront when you travel?

Chapter 10 addresses the importance of individualization. To teach special education is to be able to see the differences and uniqueness in students while maintaining ongoing alertness to changes. A special educator watches, assesses, follows intuitive signals, and then, based on findings, takes action. Consider ways you are alert to the signals around you at work and in other environments by answering the following:

1. Thinking back upon your day, what did you notice that was new or different in one of your students?
2. Where else in your life do you watch, listen, and act on your intuition?
3. Does intuitive observation and action come naturally, or have you had to develop this to do a more effective job as a special educator?

Chapter 11 focuses on the special educator's ability to problem solve. In order to provide a better education to the student with special needs, the special educator engages in the problem-solving process on a continual basis. As a special educator, you problem solve when you prioritize most important issues that need attention, when you decide on accommodations and interventions that are reasonable for this student, or when you collect data to make informed decisions and evaluate various options to select the most appropriate one. As you move forward in your profession, you will ask the following questions:

1. How do I engage in a decision-making process to provide a better option for my student?
2. How do I respond to learning differences and social behavioral problems of a student with special needs?
3. How do I determine options that are effective, feasible, and meaningful for the student with special needs?

Chapter 12 focused on collaboration. Special educators know that they work in a school that is a part of a larger community. As a special educator, you will work with various agencies and communities and will be faced with the following issues:

1. How should I work with general educators and other professionals to provide better options for my students?
2. How do I engage in co-teaching and share responsibility for planning, delivering, and evaluating instruction?
3. How do I balance my own responsibility with others in a shared decision-making process?

Chapter 13 discussed the role of the special educator as an advocate and as an individual who sees himself or herself as empowered to make a difference in the lives of students with special needs. It stressed the importance of being a lifelong learner because knowledge is power. It is critical to maintain the most current information in the field in order to be an effective advocate. As you forge ahead as an advocate for yourself and others, frequently ask yourself these questions:

1. Do I strive to maintain active involvement in my professional organization(s) so that I can keep current in the field, learn from the views of others, and stay active as a professional?
2. Do I continue to stand up for what is right even though doing so may be difficult and unpopular with some others?
3. Do I work to encourage others to advocate for themselves?

Chapter 14 discussed the importance of family involvement in a variety of ways, ranging from having positive communication and supporting the child's education to participating in a fund-raiser. When you work with families, you will create a better climate for learning, leading to positive outcomes for students with special needs. Frequently, you may ask yourself about the following situations:

1. Do I encourage family participation at every step of the special education process and view parents as a critical resource?
2. Do I create an inviting environment for parents of children in my classroom?
3. Do I ensure that I schedule meetings and other events around their convenience?

You may reflect that this is a tall order for all of the dispositions that the special educator should possess. It certainly is, yet as we think of the successful special educators that we know, they are able to fill that order and live up to the high expectations.

Our field is fortunate to have many unsung heroes who work hard every day to make a better life for students with special needs. This book salutes those individuals.

About the Authors

Beverley Holden Johns has thirty-nine years of experience working with students with learning disabilities (LD) and/or behavioral disorders (EBD) within the public schools. She supervised LD and EBD teachers in twenty-two school districts and was the founder and administrator of the Garrison Alternative School for students with severe EBD in Jacksonville, Illinois, and later the coordinator for staff development for the Four Rivers Special Education District. She is now a learning and behavior consultant and an adjunct instructor for MacMurray College (where she teaches the course on Special Education Law, on Adaptations for the General Education Classroom, and on EBD).

She chaired the Tenth Biennial Conference of the International Association of Special Education (IASE) held June 10 to 14, 2007, in Hong Kong. She serves as president of IASE (www.iase.org) in a term that extends until January 1, 2010. She presented the Inaugural Marden Lecture at the University of Hong Kong in January 2006.

Johns is the lead author of ten books (and coauthor of three others), including *Reduction of School Violence: Alternatives to Suspension*; *Techniques for Managing Verbally and Physically Aggressive Students*; *Surviving Internal Politics within the School*; *Safe Schools*; *Teacher's Reflective Calendar and Planning Journal*; *Special Educator's Reflective Calendar and Planning Journal*; *Effective Curriculum and Instruction for Students with Emotional/Behavioral Disorders*; *Students with Disabilities and General Education: A Desktop Reference for School Personnel*; *Getting Behavioral Interventions Right*; *Preparing Test-Resistant Students for Assessments: A Staff Training Guide*; *The Ethical Educator*; and *Motivating the Unmotivated Student*. She has written a workbook to accompany a video for paraprofessionals entitled *The Paraprofessional's Guide to Managing Student Behavior*, and over forty articles.

She is coauthor with Janet Lerner of the seminal college LD textbook, the 11th edition of *Learning Disabilities and Related Mild Disabilities.*

She is the 2000 recipient of the CEC Outstanding Leadership Award from the International Council for Exceptional Children, past international president (and board member until July 1, 2009) of the Council for Children with Behavioral Disorders, and the 2007 recipient of the Romaine P. Mackie Leadership Service Award.

She is listed in *Who's Who in America, Who's Who of American Women, Who's Who in American Education,* and *Who's Who among America's Teachers.* She has served as chair of Governmental Relations for several national and state organizations. She has chaired ISELA, the Illinois Special Education Coalition (whose membership includes thirteen statewide organizations) for twenty-seven years.

She is a past president of the Learning Disabilities Association of Illinois and has been the National State Presidents' Representative and served on the board of LDA of America in that role.

Johns was Jacksonville Woman of the Year in 1988, and she cochaired the Business Education Partnership Committee and the Jacksonville Truancy Task Force. She has presented workshops across the United States and Canada; in San Juan, Puerto Rico; Sydney, Australia (keynote); Warsaw, Poland; Hong Kong, China; and Lima, Peru.

She is a graduate of Catherine Spalding College in Louisville, Kentucky, and received a fellowship for her graduate work at Southern Illinois University in Carbondale, where she received an MS in special education. She has done postgraduate work at the University of Illinois, Western Illinois University, Southern Illinois University, and Eastern Illinois University.

Mary Z. McGrath taught in the Bloomington, Minnesota, public schools for thirty-one years, working as a classroom teacher, a demonstration teacher with the Project Read program, and as a special education teacher in the areas of learning disabilities, behavioral disorders, and developmental delay. She has served as national secretary for the Council for Children with Behavioral Disorders and on the board of the Minnesota Council for Exceptional Children. McGrath has a doctorate from the University of Minnesota in Educational Administration, with collateral work in organizational communication. She earned a masters' degree in educational psychology. Mary has written articles for educators, parents, caregivers, and the general public, several of which are posted on her website, http://www.maryzmcgrath.com. In addition, she has authored/coauthored books on educational subjects. She wrote *Teachers Today: A Guide to Surviving Creatively* and *Teachers in Transition: Growing Forward Through Retirement.* She is first author on *Reaching*

Students with Diverse Disabilities and *The Teacher's Reflective Calendar and Planning Journal*, as well as *The Special Educator's Reflective Calendar and Planning Journal*. She coauthored *Surviving the Internal Politics within the School* and *The Ethical Educator*. Currently, McGrath works as a professional speaker, working with schools, parents, and organizations to reflect on and improve the quality of career relationships and life transitions. She is a member of the National Speakers Association and Toastmasters International. Groups she has spoken to are listed on her website. Audiences have included Augusburg College Education Department, Minneapolis; Metro East Center, Atlanta, Georgia; Minnesota Association for Children's Mental Health; National Resource Center for Paraprofessionals; Council for Exceptional Children; Teacher Educators of Children with Behavioral Disorders; and Behavioral Institute for Children and Adolescents.

Sarup R. Mathur is a clinical professor in the College of Teacher Education and Leadership at Arizona State University. She has extensive experience in research and programming for students with emotional and behavioral disorders. She is an expert in the topics of professional development, issues of beginning special education teachers, social skills training, transition, functional behavioral assessment, and behavioral intervention plans. Her experience combines clinical and technical expertise for developing effective teacher preparation programs. At the national level, she served as the secretary and president of the Council for Children with Behavioral Disorders and the president of Teacher Educators for Children with Behavioral Disorders.